PENGUIN

HORSE RESCUE

When Joanne Schoenwald attended her first-ever knackery sale, her life changed and she devoted the next three years to rescuing horses, becoming the founder and president of Charlie's Angels Horse Rescue Inc. She is a passionate rescuer of all animals and has been changed forever by the gifts they have brought into her life. She lives on the Sunshine Coast with her husband and son and a large, diverse animal family, including seven horses that are required to do nothing except enjoy their lives. Joanne writes bestselling fiction under the name Josephine Moon.

HORSE RESCUE

Inspiring stories of second-chance horses
and the lives they changed

JOANNE SCHOENWALD

PENGUIN BOOKS

PENGUIN BOOKS

UK | USA | Canada | Ireland | Australia
India | New Zealand | South Africa | China

Penguin Books is part of the Penguin Random House group of companies whose addresses can be found at global.penguinrandomhouse.com.

First published by Penguin Random House Australia Pty Ltd, 2014
This edition published by Penguin Random House Australia Pty Ltd, 2017

10 9 8 7 6 5 4 3 2 1

Text copyright © Joanne Schoenwald 2014

The moral right of the author has been asserted.

All rights reserved. Without limiting the rights under copyright reserved above, no part of this publication may be reproduced, stored in or introduced into a retrieval system, or transmitted, in any form or by any means (electronic, mechanical, photocopying, recording or otherwise), without the prior written permission of both the copyright owner and the above publisher of this book.

Cover design by Louisa Maggio © Penguin Random House Australia Pty Ltd
Text design by Grace West © Penguin Random House Australia Pty Ltd
Cover image of Eleisha with her horse Phantom by Gavin Ifield
Typeset in Sabon by Grace West, Penguin Random House Australia Pty Ltd
Colour separation by Splitting Image Colour Studio, Clayton, Victoria
Printed and bound in Australia by Griffin Press, an accredited ISO AS/NZS 14001 Environmental Management Systems printer.

National Library of Australia
Cataloguing-in-Publication data:

    Schoenwald, Joanne, author.
    Horse rescue / Joanne Schoenwald.
    9780143572763 (paperback)
    Subjects: Horses.
    Animal rescue.
    Animal welfare.

    636.1

penguin.com.au

For my mum, Geraldine, for leading and sharing so many special animal moments with me.

CONTENTS

Introduction   1
Key Terms   3

Lincoln   5
Elf   25
Groover   43
Soul   61
Dallas   77
Horses for Hope   93
Joleena   109
Phantom   127
Astro   143
The Egyptian Horses and Donkeys   157
Boo   175
Larry   191
Salty   211
Horses I Have Known and Loved   227

Acknowledgements   245
Contacts   247

INTRODUCTION

Rescuing a single horse won't change the world for horses, but it will surely change that horse's world – Anon

When I started work on this book, I directly invited a couple of people to participate, but my major strategy to find these stories was simply to put the word out in lots of different places, via multiple means. Word of mouth did what it does best and, gradually, my inbox filled with amazing stories – stories that gave me chills, made my heart race and my spine tingle. Time and again I read these emails and wondered how so many of these fabulous stories had remained untold for so long.

The types of stories in this book are very close to my heart. Many horses have come into my life and changed me for the better. At one point, Lincoln, a horse you'll read about in this book, prompted me to found and run a horse rescue charity in southeast Queensland, which I did nearly full-time for three years. I saw some devastating things and learned more about the underworld of horse welfare in this country than I ever wanted to know. As Jacqui Steele says in her chapter, 'You open your eyes to it and it's everywhere'. Once you've seen it, you can't turn back.

But I also saw firsthand the power of healing that could be experienced not just in the rescued horse, but also in the person who becomes their custodian. And that's the book I wanted to write – one that celebrates these special bonds and unique experiences.

There is enough out there on the internet that can show you, in graphic detail, the horror and despair, and you can easily find it if you so wish. What brings me joy, what makes my heart sing, are the inspiring, goose-bumping, enlightening rescue stories of exhilarating triumph, quiet meditative wisdom, life-changing moments and powerful self-healing and self-realisation.

It is my firm belief that anyone willing to take the rescue journey with an open heart, a steady commitment, the resources and a quest for service to the animal in need, will be enriched in more ways than they can possibly imagine. I have brought together fourteen of these stories. I hope they inspire you as much as they do me.

KEY TERMS

agist/agistment: renting or leasing land and facilities to house a horse

break in/breaking in: historical term for educating a horse and beginning its experiences under saddle; many now prefer the term 'starting'

dogger: a person who slaughters horses for a variety of uses not related to human consumption; e.g. meat for pet food, as dingo bait, feed for zoo animals, fertiliser

dogger sale: a sale where horses are held in pens with numbers painted on their rumps and auctioned off to private buyers for a price ranging from ten dollars to many hundreds; unwanted horses will be taken by the dogger for slaughter

(the) dogger's: the place where horses are slaughtered for the above reason, interchangeable with the word 'knackery'

geld/gelding: a gelding is a desexed male horse; geld/gelded refers to the surgical operation by a veterinarian to desex a male horse

holding yard: locations where horses are held by horse dealers on a temporary basis while they are waiting to be sold to private buyers or sent to a knackery or slaughterhouse

horse dealer: someone who buys and sells horses for profit; can be interchangeable with the word 'dogger' because the same person often fulfils both roles

Join-Up: a process of communication with a horse, using body language; the horse is 'sent away' from the human leader, without force, until the leader uses his or her body language to invite the horse to come close willingly and stand with him or her ('join up')

knackery: there are more than thirty licensed knackeries around Australia where horses are slaughtered for a variety of uses not related to human consumption; interchangeable with the word 'dogger's'

liberty: working with a horse without the confines of ropes and sometimes without a yard

natural horsemanship: a broad term covering types of training and equine communication that favour cooperation and avoid excessive force; a recognition of a horse's instincts, psychology and behaviour as observed in wild horses; may be interchangeable with 'horse whispering'

paint: generically refers to a particular colour pattern of a horse, with large patches of white and another colour (including brown or black); may specifically refer to the breed of American Paint Horse

Parelli: a system of natural horsemanship training developed and taught by Pat Parelli in the United States

pigroot: an oppositional behaviour from a horse, similar to a small buck

slaughterhouse: the place horses are slaughtered for the purpose of exportation and human consumption

start/starting: see 'break in/breaking in'

LINCOLN

Without doubt, the horses that work in riding schools are unsung heroes.

I'm guessing that if you're reading this book, it's likely you have at least once in your life gone to a riding school, perhaps for a trail ride or some lessons. Or maybe, like me, you went for many years as a non-negotiable part of your life – a weekly ritual that fed your soul and soothed all of life's wounds; that eased your constant yearning to be with a horse and kept you off your parents' backs for a while; that left you with lifelong friends and possibly some broken bones; and that created some of the greatest highs and lows of your childhood. And perhaps, like me, you have powerful, vivid memories of that time and a good dash of nostalgia for the old days.

At my riding school, there was Barnaby, the old, flea-bitten grey plodder, who was as safe as houses and carried every beginner steadily until they found their confidence. There was Cherry, the scary Clydesdale cross, heavy enough to carry the men and the bigger people but with a sour temperament and quick, snapping teeth. There was Timbala, the flashy, sleek young paint, who broke into a satin-smooth canter and leapt effortlessly over fallen trees as you flew through the bush. There was Biggles, tall, gentle and pigeon-toed, but never stumbling. Mazina, the ex-pacer, who never trotted but wobbled you from side to side in the seat until she got into a canter. Cerise, the perfectly pretty white pony, naughty as they come but a good size for little ones on a lead line. Dee Dah, with the long, curly poodle-coat of an old horse with Cushing's disease. Molasses, the well-mannered, versatile and stunning palomino that everyone wanted and envied. Minty, a barely started pale mare that bucked me off in a public park and bolted through the suburban streets before I'd even risen from the ground. Shannon, Baghdad, Sha Tan, Oddie. I remember them all.

These were the horses that put up with me bumping around on their backs and pulling at their mouths while I found my balance. That tolerated being kicked in the sides and hit with a crop when they didn't want to move because they were tired or bored or numb to the ever-changing person on their back (and I didn't know any better). That took me into creeks, along roads, through parks, over jumps, up mountains, and through forests. That taught me how to groom and tack up, catch, feed.

Their environment taught me that a rusty bathtub filled with water could turn from a water trough into an excellent plunge pool in extreme heat, that a horse rug is a brilliant emergency jumper/windshield/groundsheet/rain sheet, and that an electric fence should be respected at all times, especially if it's wet.

These horses stood for hours while I plaited their manes

and tails. They stood solidly while I vaulted on and off their bare backs, digging my elbows in as I flailed about. They were safe(ish). They gave me confidence, joy, friendship, skills and a place to go on weekends, holidays and after school. They taught me that being in the dirt, sweating, raking up muck and sheltering under a tree when it rained was the greatest way to spend a day, and that the smells of lucerne hay, wet horses, leather saddles, damp earth and sawdust were shortcuts straight to heaven.

These riding schools become the fertile ground for so many adventures and so much personal development, especially for girls, all over the country.

But what happens to riding school horses after their usefulness has expired? Most of us wouldn't think about it much and, for people in my generation or before, the internet wasn't around for us to ask the question.

I'd heard of 'the dogger' and 'the glue factory' but I'd never had anything to do with them. And to my knowledge, no one I associated with had any either. I believed in forever homes and naively thought other people did too. Consequently, the dogger remained a bit of a myth, like the bogeyman under the bed.

So perhaps it was for this reason that, twenty years later, I responded so strongly to an email I'd received about a riding school that had closed down and was sending all of its horses to a dogger sale. I burned with outrage and righteousness. It was wrong. *Wrong*. All those horses that had given their life's work, their patience, their tolerance and suffering of inexperienced and thoughtless hands and legs, horses that had changed so many people's lives, were to be simply thrown away. It was total injustice.

I made a snap decision. My husband and I were going to that dogger sale and we were going to save a horse.

'Sold!'

The auctioneer slapped his card against his palm.

For the past several minutes my mind had been somewhere peaceful and calm, like floating on top of cool, gentle ocean waves, while my body had apparently acted of its own accord, eyes fixed straight ahead and hand rising in the air again and again.

But now I slammed back into my body, instantly and regrettably aware of the intense heat that pummelled us from above and hit the rough, chequered cement at our feet and bounced straight back up our legs. I was pressed against the hard wooden rail of the pen behind me. My feet, legs and lower back ached from the hours we'd been standing like this in the middle of the day on a concrete floor. There was a deep pain in my chest, making it difficult to breathe.

'What happened?' I said.

A cast of faces swayed around me, with red cheeks, broad-brimmed cattleman's hats, bulbous noses and cauliflower ears.

The bidders closest to me laughed. The mass of bodies totally filled the width of the walkway between the rows of pens containing hundreds of miserable horses, all with blue painted numbers on their rumps to identify them but nothing more – no person to represent them, no loved one saying goodbye, no information on their history or why they were there. I couldn't have escaped the crush at that moment even if I'd wanted to.

My jeering neighbours pointed towards the bidding pen,

an area I couldn't even see due to the sheer volume of people and wide hats standing between me and whatever lay on the other side.

'You bought *that* one!'

I bent down, hoping to see what they were pointing at from between jeans and brass-buckled hips. I could make out blackish dirty horse legs, two sets of them by the look of it, but nothing else.

'Was it the pony?'

I vaguely remembered hearing the auctioneer describe a pony and thinking maybe a pony would be a good idea.

'No. The black horse.' More laughter.

I turned to Alwyn. Nausea flipped my stomach.

'What happened?' The bidding card was crumpled in my damp palm.

His eyes bore into mine. I'll never forget his eyes in that instant – the purest moment of unconditional love and total acceptance of whatever crazy journey I was about to lead him on.

He gave me a small, sympathetic smile. He was drenched in sweat, great pools of it soaking his dark shirt and running down his temples. It took him a moment to find words.

'You just bought a horse.'

Yes, I had. But it was an accident.

By this time of my life, I'd had horses for twenty years. And here I was at my first ever dogger auction and, apparently, I'd just bought a horse.

Whether it was the heat stroke, the sheer emotional overwhelm of the day, or divine intervention, I'd bought Lincoln. And it was Lincoln who led me to commit the next three years of my life to nearly full-time voluntary service rescuing dozens of horses just like him.

We had no horse transport ourselves but had been told we could organise something when we got to the saleyards. The only transport we could find was a cattle truck and the driver told us it would cost the same amount to get back to our place whether we got one horse or ten. We'd already walked the aisles of the hundreds of horses on death row, most of them in awful condition – again, something I'd never seen before – and quickly agreed to take home four. The thought of leaving even one of them behind was devastating but we thought we could handle four and we would work out what to do with them after we got home.

By the time Alwyn and I had made it to the end of the auction, we'd bought four horses. I still hadn't even seen Lincoln; we'd had to move on with the crush of bidders down the packed alleyway between the pens. We had his number written down on the back of the bidding card and we counted the pens and numbers until we found his and stopped at the gate.

'Oh my God!'

They were the first words out of my mouth and the only words I could say for several moments. I stood in horror in front of him. I'd never seen a horse in that kind of condition before. I'd lived in a world where people loved their horses and took care of them. I couldn't believe I had been so naive. And Lincoln wasn't alone. There were two hundred horses at that auction and many of them looked like him, coming out of a long, hard winter on the back of a drought.

I quickly took in his appearance. *Bones*. That was my first thought. *I can see his bones. Everywhere.* I could see every vertebra in his spine. Ribs. Pelvis. In horse language, he would be assessed as having a body-condition score of one and a half. The scale runs from zero to five, with five being obese. Years later, I intervened in a rescue of a horse with a condition score of zero with the only way I could, paying for a vet to euthanase her because she was too far gone. As it was, when the vet arrived she'd fallen to the ground and couldn't get up again.

But Lincoln sat at one and a half. The extra half a point was because his neck, while thin, hadn't yet turned to a U-shape; it was still straight along the top. Today, Lincoln's mane is long, thick and lustrous. That day, there was barely any there, just a few centimetres of it, brittle and dull. Perhaps it had fallen out or broken off due to malnutrition, or perhaps a fellow paddock-mate had chewed on it in desperation for food. The remains of his winter coat, such as it had been, clung helplessly in thin, crackling patches. His skin was flaking and he was covered in sores. There was a large crack in one of his front hooves. He shrank to the back of the pen under the double-barrelled kicking blows of the black pony that shared the space, simply too exhausted to defend himself.

After I'd recovered from the shock of Lincoln's condition, my thoughts turned to action.

'Well, thank God you came to me,' I said to him. And with those words, my life changed.

I pulled back the wooden slide bolt on the gate and stepped inside with a halter in hand, a foolish action I now think. He could very easily have turned on me in that confined space. I knew nothing about him and, as I came to learn later on, the dogger pens are full of horses that have had traumatic experiences and turned to dangerous behaviour to defend themselves.

He immediately raised his head, snorted and stepped as far back as the wooden rails would let him go.

'Whoa,' I said, lowering the halter. I ignored the pony and maintained my connection to this terrified black horse, willing him to trust me.

I approached slowly, holding out my hand for him to sniff, and then moved to his side to stroke his neck. He stiffened, but I kept stroking and talking to him, and he turned his nose to me, sniffing my arms. Suddenly, he let out a big sigh and lowered his head and rested his forehead on my chest, right over my heart, holding it there, perfectly still.

People say you shouldn't attribute human emotions to animals. But at that moment I was flooded with waves of undeniable *thank you* gratitude from Lincoln. It was then, and still remains, one of the most powerful moments of my life.

I looked up at Alwyn on the other side of the rails and tears sprang to my eyes. I would never be the same again.

The emotional high of rescuing four horses quickly turned to stress for the practical realities. I began begging other people at the saleyard for food for the four horses we'd bought and I was particularly worried Lincoln might not even make it home. The cattle truck was a far-from-ideal way to transport horses, especially ones that were weak and frightened and who might fight with each other, hit their heads on the bars above them, and slip and slide on the metal floor during the two-hour winding journey home. And we didn't have a cattle ramp at our property so they would have to jump off the back of the truck in the dark later that night.

All of these logistical issues, combined with the exceptional shock of what we'd seen at the sales, the stress of not knowing what to do with these horses once we got them home to our place (we already had three horses and only six acres of land), and the whole mind- and body-altering experience of stepping into 'the real world' of horse welfare had irrevocably affected us. We couldn't un-see what we'd seen.

We wouldn't be able to properly assess them until the next morning in daylight. We'd taken home one of the ex-riding school horses that we'd originally gone to save – a middle-aged grey mare who appeared to be a Thoroughbred and who came with her weathered leather bridle and saddle attached. Alwyn named her Lily. She had a massive injury up her back leg, with a huge amount of skin removed and purple antiseptic spray all over it as a token treatment. She was thin, but not critical, and she found a home the very next day with someone we knew in the local area. We also brought home a ten-year-old Thoroughbred mare I named Rosie, who was absolutely delightful and appeared to be in very good health. She went to a new home fairly quickly as well, where, it was discovered, she was extremely 'girthy' (reacting with opposition when the girth to hold the saddle on was presented or tightened) and needed some patient retraining to help her on her way, which she received from her new family. Rosie went on to take many happy children to pony club adventures.

That left us with a scrawny colt I'd called Charlie, who was less than two years old, and Lincoln. The day after he arrived, I noticed that Charlie had a small injury to one of his back fetlocks, a tiny wound that looked as though he'd copped a kick from one of the other horses overnight. He wasn't very lame so I treated it topically. He was set to go to a foster home with a friend of a friend who'd said she'd happily take a pony on temporarily to find it a new home. A couple of days later, though, he was getting more lame and I said to the foster carer when she came to pick him up that I thought she should call the vet as soon as possible. By the time he'd finished his two-hour journey home he was horrendously lame. X-rays revealed the small wound was actually a puncture wound and he had a fracture in the joint requiring several thousand dollars worth of surgery, or euthanasia.

Meanwhile, I'd now named Lincoln, after Abraham Lincoln. I felt it was a fitting name for him because I was certain down to my bones that he would go on to be some sort of spokesman for emaciated and suffering horses everywhere. At the very least, he needed a name of strength to pull him through. I had him on four-hourly feeds because I didn't know when he'd last had any real food, or for how long his gut had been empty, and the risk of colic was high.

But I remember thinking, that first day at home, as I trundled across the lawn with yet another feed for Lincoln, that there surely couldn't be anything more important in the world at that moment than feeding this horse and ending his suffering. I wrote about it on a blog and people began responding straight away. Lincoln's message of hope was already getting out into the world.

As bad timing goes, Alwyn and I were packing to head to Tonga for a week to swim with the humpback whales. It was well and truly a terrible time to rescue four horses and certainly not a good time to get the news that the pony needed surgery. But, as

I would come to discover in the next three years, animal rescues rarely happen at a good time and the faster I could accept that my life was now in service to them, not the other way around, the easier it would make my decisions.

Since we still legally owned the pony, it was up to us to make the decision and come up with the money.

In the middle of finding passports and organising everything for our house-sitter to deal with our menagerie of animals, Alwyn and I made a decision – we didn't just pull this pony out of a dogger yard simply to give up on him now. We would find a way to make the surgery happen and, fortunately, some good friends joined the efforts to spread the word for the need for help.

That was a big organisational drama to deal with. But my emotional attention was with Lincoln. He had swellings around his chest, which the vet said was from leaked fluid from the muscle he was breaking down to survive; a sign things were indeed very bad. And he was so utterly terrified of people that he wouldn't let me do anything other than put a halter on him. If I tried to take a step towards his shoulder he simply spun in circles so his nose was facing me the whole time. He used his front legs to strike while the vet assessed him and had alarming overreactions to anything that frightened him. Today, Lincoln can still be reactive to some stimuli but, looking back on it, I think his nerves were just shot, both from the trauma and from the nutritional deficiencies.

He was the first emotionally and behaviourally difficult horse I'd had to deal with. I even said to Alwyn in those early days that maybe it would be kinder to euthanase him because he seemed so out of his mind with fear and was in such a poor physical state. But as far as his behaviour went, I had to relegate him to the 'too hard' basket for the moment and concentrate on getting to Tonga and also helping the pony with his broken fetlock.

Our journey to Tonga was a long one with many stopovers in airports. I sat at internet terminals and wrote articles and press releases for newspapers telling Charlie's story and asking people if they wished to help us pay for this pony's surgery. Somewhere along the line I began saying, 'Could you be Charlie's angel?'

Charlie had his surgery to fix his fetlock and came through with no ongoing issues. He was also gelded and his foster carer eventually decided she couldn't let him go. We'd raised about two-thirds of his surgery costs and Alwyn and I paid the rest.

Alwyn and I talked a lot about the rescue horses while we were in Tonga and we both firmly believed that we'd been at that saleyard for a reason. We'd seen things we'd never seen before and could not go on with our eyes closed. We believed there were no accidents, that for some reason I'd been meant to buy Lincoln, and that we'd been called to higher action. We decided we needed to start a horse rescue charity so we could continue to help horses like Lincoln and Charlie and the hundreds of others that went through the horse sales every weekend in this country looking for their last chance. My experience of facing the darkness of the sales head on, and then raising funds for Charlie, convinced me I could do it. I called the charity Charlie's Angels Horse Rescue Inc. to continue the momentum we'd started with Charlie's publicity.

But it was Lincoln who challenged me beyond my limits. Once again, I realised how sheltered I'd been. I'd had a beautiful 17-hand-high Thoroughbred, Hercules, for sixteen years, followed by Trav, Jum Jum and Leila – all completely gentle, unchallenging horses. I'd never had to work through a 'problem horse' before and I felt completely out of my depth.

Physically, Lincoln began to recover well. He had youth on his side, and remained on high rations for weeks to get his gut moving again and to halt the downward spiral. He lay down a lot in those first few days, sleeping in the sun, something I noticed frequently in future rescue horses that had been through that kind of prolonged starvation and exhaustion. The crack in his hoof has never healed, despite all our best efforts, but it's manageable as long as he gets regular trimming and the weather is kind. Other than that, he's now a very healthy, robust horse, and one that is a very 'good doer' – he really does not need much food to survive at all, which always makes me wonder what sort of hell he'd been through to get into the condition he was in.

As his physicality returned, so did his fight and will to live. He began asserting his dominance over my timid, gentle Arabs, quickly rising to the top of the herd. (It's a place he held over every other horse that came through our property in the following three years, with the exception of Joleena and Shona, who'll you'll read about later in this book.) Despite his fears, Lincoln was affectionate with me, but still wouldn't let me pass his shoulder, not even with my hand. I'd spent a long time brushing him very gently with a soft brush to remove all the skin flakes and scabs on his neck, and the blooming summer coat underneath all that dead hair meant he'd started to show his handsome genes.

He didn't eat carrots, another thing I later found with a lot of rescue horses, as though no one had ever bothered to give them a treat. My mare, Jum Jum, had been the same when she first arrived with us and so I did the same thing I'd done with her and began slicing them and putting them in with his chaff for him to experiment with. It's certainly not essential for a horse to eat carrots but it's a tasty treat for them and works wonders when building a relationship.

One afternoon, Lincoln was eating his dinner and I had a carrot in my hand. I broke off a piece and tossed it into the rubber feed bin but it bounced straight up onto his nose. Lincoln's immediate response was not to flee, as most horses would, but to strike with both feet, one after the other. It is often his first response to any situation of stress. Fight first, flee later. He carries a number of scars around his hooves and legs, and at first I thought he'd perhaps gotten caught frequently in fencing, but my experiences with him suggest something else. Lincoln is an exceptionally social horse and talks over the fence to any other animal or any person who'll talk to him and, hence, does actually get caught in fences just through his enthusiasm for engagement. But he doesn't struggle to get free. Not at all. He waits, standing perfectly still – once even for a whole day before I found him, if the amount of manure next to him was anything to go by.

These three things – his stand-still-and-fight behaviour, the scars up his legs, and the fact that I know he can stand still for many hours at a time, suggest to me that he was perhaps hobbled in his past (tying a horse's legs together to prevent them moving around). Most vets agree he's likely a stock horse, and he will 'ground tie' with a rope hanging to the ground but he doesn't tether to a fence, something else that adds to this picture.

This learned fighting behaviour made Lincoln a scary prospect for me. But again, I felt I'd been given an opportunity to do more. So I persisted. His first big breakthroughs came when I called a Bowen therapist in my area to see if she would treat him.

She came pro bono and worked with Lincoln and it was the first time he began to let us move past his shoulders. Though he was nervous at first, with some striking at the ground in warning, she gently worked through his resistance until his head began to drop and big sighs were released. She kept coming, teaching him that people could not only be nice but actually bring relief and comfort too. Lincoln began to welcome her enthusiastically.

Now I could work around his body, still carefully, but I could brush him all over and begin to experiment with rugs and saddles. He carries a white scar on his wither that is most likely a saddle scar, the result of someone riding him in a painful, ill-fitting saddle. Lincoln bucked the first time I put a soft saddle on him, careering and bucking around the yard as an instant reaction to try to dislodge this thing he'd come to associate with pain, until he realised it didn't hurt any more. He did it again the second time I put a saddle on him, but with far less enthusiasm. And after that he seemed to realise the old experience of the painful saddle was in his past.

Still, he was nervous and reactive and beyond my abilities. I knew I needed help. As so often happened when running a horse rescue charity, the perfect person approached at just the right moment. Katrina, a student of the horsemanship school of Parelli, phoned and offered her services to any of our horses that might need it. She began working with Lincoln. In their first meeting, as she was trying to catch him, he leapt into the air and kicked her. But she still finished the session saying she'd like to adopt him. She was the perfect person for him. But it forced me to assess my feelings about Lincoln and I knew I'd been kidding myself. There was no way I could let him go. He and I had a strong connection, one I hadn't gone looking for, one that wasn't easy, was often challenging and occasionally frightening, but always rewarding.

He was the horse that took me into learning more about Parelli and the whole field of horse–human communication, which seems to be at the root cause of all horse 'problems'. He opened my eyes to the intensive journey so many rescue horses recovering from trauma and neglect have to go on. Whenever things got tough running the charity, as they frequently did, all I had to do was think of Lincoln, of where he came from, how he'd changed, and how he'd changed me, and I knew it was worth it.

At about the same time, I began to study Equine Facilitated Learning (EFL), which is working with horses and people (often children or people with illnesses or special needs) and Equine Assisted Psychotherapy (EAP). I also went to New Zealand to study with the American group, EAGALA. The course was fascinating, but what it did for me more than anything else was to affirm that horses were 'valuable' and 'useful' simply because they exist. Just by being themselves, horses were a reservoir of healing potential waiting to be tapped. It deepened my belief even more so that rescue horses had much to offer humanity.

We talked a lot in that course about the types of horses that made good therapy horses and, while almost all horses are suitable, the instructors advised that any known to be biters or kickers should be avoided. As Lincoln had already kicked someone, that ruled him out.

After I returned to Australia, a family came to our house for an EFL session. I had a nice safe yard set up and put Sparky, a rescued Shetland pony, in there. Sparky is one of those wonderful 'bombproof' ponies and I thought he'd be suitable for the two foster children who were coming; the girl was seven and the boy eight years of age. The boy had recently been expelled from school for bullying behaviour. He was very high energy, low on concentration, and moved rapidly around Sparky, who didn't care one bit about that and so I knew the boy was quite safe.

I gave the children some activities to do, brushing Sparky and leading exercises, both alone and as a team, but after about half an hour, the boy wanted to connect with the big horses who were on the other side of the fence. Lincoln was standing closest, watching what was going on (as usual, seeking engagement). The boy ran straight at Lincoln with grass in his hand. Lincoln, not like Sparky at all and highly reactive, reared backwards and ran away. The boy was shocked, a little upset, and banged on the fence, which of course made Lincoln go even further.

I said to him, 'Why do you think Lincoln ran away?'

'I dunno,' was his immediate response. I waited a beat and then he said, 'He was scared.'

'Oh. I see. What do you think you could do differently to make him feel safe?'

'I dunno!' Again, I waited. And he said, 'Stand still.'

'Okay. Do you want to try that?'

So he went and stood at the fence, still for the first time since he'd arrived, and held out his grass through the wire for Lincoln. Lincoln watched him for a few moments, ears pricked, and then walked up to him. I was thrilled and so was the boy. Lincoln, by his very reactivity, had just given the boy a powerful lesson about how to approach people and read their body language and sensitivity, something Sparky couldn't do because Sparky would never react like that. It was Lincoln, not Sparky, who was his best teacher that day.

One of the greatest joys in having Lincoln has been to see his personality emerge from beneath the layers of fear and uncertainty. He is a very mouthy horse, not especially in a biting sense, but he communicates with his nose and lips. Everything goes in his mouth, something many horse trainers dislike but it's a trait that actually makes him very accessible to people. He sniffs, nibbles, breathes, kisses, tickles and smooches. He will untie shoelaces, has been known to undo belts and scarves, and steals anything left on the ground. Once, when I'd badly sprained my ankle, I sat down on a log in the paddock for a rest and he came and stole my crutches, dragging the yellow sticks across the red dirt while I yelled at him to bring them back to me.

He has earned the nicknames of 'the Italian stallion' or 'the black stallion', even though he's a gelding. He has a powerful masculine seductiveness that wins over all the mares (and many women as he nuzzles their ears). His gelding hasn't affected his desire to connect with mares and express his passions physically, much to the embarrassment of many visitors and children, who get a quick lesson in equine reproduction behaviour.

The charity was asked to appear on the children's television show *Totally Wild* a couple of times, and for one of the episodes the camera crew came to my property to film a feature story. A friend and I washed and groomed all the horses on our property (eight of them, at the time) and covered them in rugs to keep them clean until the next day. But when the crew arrived, they were so utterly taken with Lincoln – who insisted on thoroughly inspecting the presenter, the camera and the microphone with his nose, and providing such an endearing performance – that all other horses were passed over for more footage of the black gelding who just loved people.

I have a lot of 'draw' with Lincoln. That is, he connects to me immediately and will follow me closely if I engage him, often with his nose on my back or burrowed in my hair (which is a bit disturbing and I tend to ask him to back off). So it was easy enough to have him follow me around the round yard for the camera, over and over again as they took their many minutes of footage. I could ask him to circle the yard at liberty, continuing at a trot until I gave him a hand signal to stop, and turn in towards me, and he did it over and over again, perfectly for each take. Over the years, Lincoln appeared in several magazines and newspapers and did indeed become the 'voice' I imagined he would when I gave him his name in those early days.

In the beginning, I'd doubted my ability to help a horse like Lincoln. But as each new rescue came my way, and as I inevitably came into contact with horses even tougher than Lincoln, I would only need to snuggle with my lovely boy and remind myself that once upon a time I thought I couldn't do it. But I was wrong. I could do that and more.

It seems like a dream to me, now, thinking of that terrified, emaciated, crazed horse that set my adrenaline pounding with his hysterical reactions to the smallest things. Today, Lincoln is calm (generally), funny and a much-loved horse, and there isn't a single person who comes to visit who doesn't spend time with him and leave with a beaming face. Lincoln is tactile and affable and breaks down people's resistant walls as though they're made of paper. Even non-horse people love Lincoln, and he facilitates this with his nosey, mouthy, in-your-face ways. I, of course, adore all my horses but there is something about Lincoln that touches my heart in a way no other horse does. He presented me with the chance to leap, to feel the fear and do it anyway, and be rewarded to discover that the net did indeed appear to catch me. He taught me to have faith.

ELF

Elf is a child's pony dream come true. At just three feet in height, with a white coat and dark black eyes, a long, thick mane and tail, pricked ears that always show interest in whatever's going on around him, and inquisitive lips that greet every person he meets with tactile, warm kisses, he is heart-stoppingly, criminally gorgeous.

Jill Strachan and I sit inside the front window of her house with a cup of coffee and pore over the hundreds of photos on her computer, squealing and gushing as only horse lovers can.

Suddenly she says, 'I think I'm obsessed.'

Jill has many horses on her property but Elf is her first ever pony.

'I came over from Scotland when I was five. We were ten-pound Poms. I'd had a couple of sits on a pony when I was over there and loved it, just loved it, but didn't realise how much I loved it and neither did my parents until I was five or six years old and we went to the Royal Easter Show. We walked into the horse stalls and I stuck my head in there and took a huge breath in and realised I loved that smell! And that's what it's been like my whole life; it's a sensory thing. I smell my horses every day, I love the smell of hay and sawdust . . . and I always wanted a pony.'

Elf is her childhood dream come true. 'He's everything a little kid would love. He's got an infectious personality. He's very much like a cheeky kid. And people look at me and they just laugh because he's my child. Elf can do no wrong. He makes me laugh all the time. I laugh more since Elf's been with me than I ever did before. He brings out the child in me. There's more joy, more fun, more laughter. How could there not be? Look at him!'

But this dream pony's life could well have ended in a nightmare.

If Jill hadn't told me she was a teacher, I would have guessed. She exudes the kind of qualities so often found in good teachers who have worked in the education system for many years and still find joy in what they do. She's patient, calm, a clear thinker and problem solver. When you're in Jill's presence you can relax because it's clear someone else has got it all covered.

But that *togetherness* falls away the second I ask Jill if she remembers where she was when she first heard about Elf.

'I remember being here on Christmas Day. I had my mum up from Sydney, and it was that really rainy time just prior to the January 2011 Queensland floods, so we'd been inside and we'd had a few wines, as you do, and the news came on. As soon as I heard, "There's been an incident with a pony . . . a pony's been dragged," I said, "Sorry, I can't watch that," and turned it off. I said, "No, no, no, this isn't happening, somebody did *not* drag a pony with a car."'

Two men from Murphy's Creek near Toowoomba in Queensland had tied the pony to their car and driven along Murphy's Creek Road. The pony, obviously unable to keep up with the car, fell to the road but the driver kept going, dragging him at speed and causing horrific injuries and terror until a member of the public confronted them and called the police.

'The next day, because of all the rain and subsequent problems, my little colt was incredibly ill. He was about six weeks old, and we had to get him into the vet's or else he was going to die. He was colicky and he was just dropping like you wouldn't believe. So we got him into the vet's, got him sedated and got him calm and then I hear over the loudspeaker, "That pony that was dragged by the car is on its way in." I thought, *No, no, we don't want to see this; it's going to be awful.*'

So both Jill and her husband, Paul Williams, left Redlands Veterinary Clinic and went home. But despite Jill's efforts to shut out any knowledge of the pony on Christmas Day and again on Boxing Day 2011, fate had other ideas.

'When we went back to the vet's to visit our colt, Elf was there. He was in a stall and shaking all over from the shock, with bandages everywhere.' She grimaces. 'They were taking the bandages off to assess him, and the *smell* . . . that rotting, putrid smell. If you've got horses, you know the smell.'

Elf had been seized by the RSPCA but they didn't have the facilities to deal with the type of injuries and the level of care he needed, so they asked veterinarian David Lovell to take him.

'Elf needed intensive care and David's one of the leading

experts in legs, so if you've got a leg problem you go to David. So I was there and, I don't know why, but I thought, *I'm just going to go over and say hello*.

'I went over and knelt down next to him. He was still shaking. I said, "Hi, mate," and he turned and looked at me in the eyes and there was this really powerful connection. He connected to me. And I thought, *Wow! Here's a horse who's been through intense trauma and he can still connect to people. That's really special*.

'And then one of the nurses said, "His name is Elf." And I went still inside.'

In March 2010, Jill had started a not-for-profit organisation called Equine Learning for Futures – ELF – as a way of combining her work as a special needs teacher with her passion for horses. Through ELF, she works with disadvantaged and at-risk youth as well as those with learning difficulties and those going through trauma.

And now here was a tiny pony that had been through intense trauma and still had a long road of healing ahead, who didn't have a home to go to, and his name was Elf. The staff had named him that because he was so small and because it was Christmas. But for Jill his name was a big, flashing sign.

'I didn't say anything. I didn't say anything for a long time. It was weeks later that I mentioned the possibility of me adopting him to David, and the RSPCA were really positive about the type of work Elf could be doing in our organisation, so they agreed.'

In another incredible twist of fate, Murphy's Creek was one of the worst hit areas of the January 2011 floods, in which three quarters of Queensland was declared a disaster zone. Thirty-five people died, including twenty-one from the Lockyer Valley, of which Murphy's Creek is a part. The paddock Elf had lived in prior to his attack was inundated. Had the Christmas Day attack not happened, he would most certainly have drowned.

So how does Jill make sense of all these coincidences – of twice running away from wanting to know anything about Elf; of her colt falling ill and being rushed to hospital at the same time Elf was coming to the surgery; of his name being the same as her organisation's; of the fact that Elf would likely have died in the floods just a couple of weeks later if this hadn't happened at all?

'It was just supposed to be. It felt so right when I met him. It was absolutely amazing.'

Elf came home to Jill around six weeks after his attack. His injuries were so severe that euthanasia had been considered as a treatment option but the vets decided to give him a chance.

'I remember watching him in the early weeks when he was lying down a lot, wracked with pain and thinking maybe they should just put him down and put him out of his misery. But then the next day he got up. He wasn't ready to give in.'

Elf's knees were torn open, right down to the joints, the legacy of which is fusion of one of the knee joints. His pasterns – the area between the hoof and the fetlocks (the first major joint above the hoof) were torn open too. His back feet were torn and bloodied, the pedal bones (the bone inside the hoof) fractured. Pieces of bone were still coming out after Jill got him home. From those injuries, it's not hard to imagine the position he must have been in while being dragged: fallen on both front knees and legs, his head wrenched upwards and tied to the car, with his back feet braced along the bitumen in his desperate attempts to stop and get back up on his front feet.

Amazingly, Elf seems to suffer no ongoing health issues. He walked with a limp for a long time while the knee joint was fusing, but once it fused it became more stable. Jill does worry about his weight, though. Miniature ponies are very 'good doers', seeming to live off the smell of an oily rag. They gain weight easily and it can be difficult to get it off again once it's there. Elf's dietary needs are so different from the large Thoroughbreds that surround him at his new home that it can be challenging to keep him to his diet, especially when he's so clever and cheeky. He can't wander freely through the many acres of grass because he would gain weight too quickly. Instead, he has a section of very short grass roped off around the five stables where he spends his time and nibbles at a few blades between feeds.

'I have to have eyes in the back of my head to make sure he doesn't just run under the big horses' legs. This pony has caused havoc on so many occasions when I haven't been watching. He vacuums the big horses' stables. He goes straight to the 28-year-old's stable because Sammy gets a bran mash and he might have left some. I have to race ahead and make sure there's none there because that will make Elf sick.'

Founder is a very serious and painful hoof condition that can affect any horse but is more common in overweight horses and all ponies and is the second-biggest killer of horses after colic. It can make anyone nervous at the best of times but since Elf's hooves were damaged in his attack it adds another level of concern for the integrity of his pedal bones. On the day I visit, Elf's just been put on a diet of soaked hay, a method that leaches the sugars out of the hay and into the water, leaving a lower-calorie hay behind for sugar-sensitive horses.

Elf's new home with Jill is a former rose farm set on twelve acres, with a just a few rose beds left in the house yard and the rest of the property devoted to horses. Jill and Paul also lease another fourteen acres of a neighbouring property to give them more room for the average of seventeen horses that reside at the property, with more out in race training at any given time. Paul is on the board of Brisbane Racing and has a small interest in breeding racehorses at their property, and Jill commits to each horse for its life, so most retire on their property.

She works with her retired racehorses as well as Elf in equine-assisted learning programs.

'The program teaches communication, behaviour modification, controlling emotions, a lot of self-confidence and giving students the time to process information.'

Work with the horse on the ground might lead to riding skills if the horse and client are able and well matched for that.

'I've seen the power of a little person being up high and being in control, being able to decide to go here or go there. Motor skills are also developed this way, through the movement of the horse, through balance and finding their body, holding their core stability, and all those other physical developments that go with riding. We're not doing what we do to teach horsemanship; we're doing it for their growth and development. Some kids are physically unable to get on a horse. But if they're able and they want to – it's always their choice – I will get them up on a horse.'

Jill's had to train Elf differently to the way she's trained her Thoroughbreds before this. She worked intensively for a year to 'clicker train' Elf, giving small food rewards after he performs a correct move, anchored by the noise of the clicker. One of his developing talents is painting original artworks.

Elf is a very 'mouthy' pony. He loves to put everything in his mouth, whether that's food, T-shirts, hoses, hats or a paintbrush. It is a constant balancing act for Jill to teach him horsemanship manners while not suppressing all his personality and natural desires to connect with people by nuzzling and licking and chewing, which can open the door for a shy child to open up and connect with him. Jill decided to channel that mouthiness and teach him to paint, in the hope that Elf's paintings could one day create a stream of income for the charity.

On this day, Jill clips a big sheet of white paper to a wooden board and leans it against a post near the stable. She starts by offering the handle of the paintbrush to Elf and when he takes it she clicks her clicker, he looks away (which is the trained, appropriate response to ensure they are respectful around food), and then she hands him his reward. Then she asks him to target the page – touch his nose to the paper. *Click. Reward.* She dips his paintbrush in blue paint and offers it to him again. *Click. Reward.* Then he's asked to paint. He streaks the brush across the paper and then drops it. *Click. Reward.*

He's offered the brush several more times, and then offered a mini roller, and he takes it and targets the paper and brushes across it, sometimes moving back and forth. It's a messy work in progress at this stage. And because he likes to chew, he often breaks the handle of his painting tool, crunching it between those powerful front teeth. Sometimes he tears the paper. Jill is still experimenting with the consistency of the paints, the type of canvas he can paint on and the types of tools he can work with before munching his way through them all. But at the end of this session, we have an abstract blue work of art in progress. Jill says she might let it dry and then add a different colour to it later.

Then she shows me how he can count with his front hoof, pawing at the earth in successive movements. And he can shake his head to say 'no'.

Not everyone who comes for an ELF session will work with Elf the pony. That will depend on Jill's sense of what the client needs and which of her horses might best deliver it. But most people who come already know about Elf.

'For traumatised kids I explain to them what's happened to him and I say, "Now he'd like to help you, would you like to work with him?" And of course they do.' Elf's ability to transcend boundaries and emotional walls can't be overestimated.

I ask Jill about her world view, whether or not she thinks there is a grand plan for us all.

'I believe in all that stuff. I don't seek it. But I accept it. Ever since I was a child, I have wanted to do something. I wanted to make a difference. That's why I got into teaching, because I realised I could make a difference. I want to do something with my life and it makes me feel really good to do that.'

Whenever an opportunity comes along, she embraces it, as was the case with Elf.

'I knew I had to do something for this little pony. I had to make it *right*. I knew he would be a mascot. I knew his story needed to be told and that we had the opportunity to make a big wrong right and do something new and walk another path.'

Jill says she fell into special needs teaching. She'd developed chronic fatigue syndrome working full-time as a high school teacher and had to take extended sick leave. The Department of Education then offered her a part-time role in a primary school within the special needs unit, an unexpected opportunity she embraced and now looks back on as a big blessing.

'If you looked at my life pathway you'd see I was destined to do this.'

Apart from being a special needs teacher for intellectually impaired, autistic and traumatised students, Jill's personal story gives clear insight into why she does what she does *and* why she's so good at it.

'I came from a broken family. I was a very, very naughty child and teenager. Absolute rebellion.'

Then, at the age of fourteen, Jill woke up one day and knew she needed to change her life, a moment of incredible self-awareness for one so young.

'It was like a little neuron fired. I knew that if I didn't stop, I'd end up in jail. And I thought, no, I can do something with my life. It was hard. It was hard being naughty and doing the wrong things. I had to relearn how to do the right things.

'Mum was obviously in the picture but being a fourteen year old is all about you, so you don't necessarily see how your actions are affecting everyone else. So this thing about wanting to change was all about me. I didn't want to be in trouble any more. I didn't want to feel at risk. When I was with the people around me in my group, I felt scared physically and emotionally, scared that I would be kidnapped or raped. I was putting myself into situations that weren't healthy. I knew it was wrong but I did it anyway. So I decided I wasn't going to do it any more.'

Jill and her mum moved a few months later to another part of Sydney and a new school offered the fresh start she was looking for. But it still wasn't a clear run. She spent too much time playing cards and socialising during school and repeated Year 12 simply out of sheer determination to continue to improve her life, believing if she didn't go to university then she'd have few choices in life.

'So I went back to the same high school and repeated Year 12. I can still remember walking down those steps . . . it was awful. It was *awful*. How many times I've had to suck my pride in and say to myself, "You know what? They can't affect me because if I don't do this, then I don't get over there, and I want to get over there. So suck it up, girl, this is what you've got to do."'

It was a brave thing to do.

'Yeah, I suppose,' she says. 'I'm surprised when people give up so easily. I don't understand it. I'm a fighter. I always take on a challenge. Always. If it's not a challenge, it's not worth doing. I'm just not interested if it's easy. I've got to push myself.'

Her determination paid off. She went to university and studied teaching for four years and thoroughly enjoyed it, graduating as a high school teacher. Some wonderful years of teaching followed, where she worked with students who 'weren't quite coping' and Jill's dream of doing something with her life seemed to be finally coming together. But on a personal level, she was struggling in a difficult marriage.

'It's really interesting, you know, you see all these people and they seem really well put together but they go home and they're in these abusive relationships and situations. I remember, there was one night, and he was just on at me, on at me, on at me, on at me. We would fight all the time. Fight, fight, fight, fight, fight. And I thought, if he does that again, I'm taking a knife and I'm stabbing myself. And then I thought, that's not very healthy!'

Jill's inner wisdom led her to seek help with a professional who advised her to leave her marriage immediately. 'She said, "Do yourself and your husband a favour and leave now." So I did.'

Brave again.

'I moved away. Left my life. Left everything behind. All my friends. Even my dog. I tried taking the dog but it didn't work. But I always took the feeling with me that the further I got away from that house, the better I felt.'

Finally, Jill was free to question what she really wanted to do. She decided to remake her life. That led to physical adventures, including a five-day ride of the Snowy Mountains.

And that's where she met her future husband, Paul Williams, twenty-two years ago.

'Horses brought us together.'

Paul had never been a rider and that Snowy Mountain trek was his first ride on a horse.

'He was so sore! Alcohol helped,' she laughs. 'That and jumping into the Jindabyne River.'

They were both very shy with each other on that trip but Paul tracked down Jill's address and handwrote her a letter, which she still has today, along with the six months' worth of letters that followed.

It was time to draw on even more courage. She packed up her life once more and moved from Sydney to Queensland to be with him and start over yet again.

Working with troubled youth was still her calling and all her teaching roles seemed to lead in this direction.

'I understand what they have to go through. When you're in that place . . . you can do things and you don't care about the consequences because nothing anyone can do to you hurts as much as you feel inside. Nothing.'

Jill can still get emotional about the pain she went through in her younger days but knows it made her what she is today and gave her the empathy and understanding to work with others in crisis. She feels she's healed from those experiences.

Perhaps not so, though, for the ten years she and Paul spent enduring IVF cycles.

'That is really hard to heal. I'm comfortable 95 per cent of the time. But it will always hurt.'

It's a testament to their marriage that they came through that and are still so strong.

'We look at each other now and we say, well, nothing is as bad as that.'

Although she now loves her job as a special needs teacher, Jill says it took a long time to grow into it, devoting herself to self-directed learning in this new field and being patient with herself while she figured out how to do a good job.

Her understanding of natural horsemanship helped a lot.

'Horses don't generalise and often these kids don't either. So, for example, you might work with a horse at one spot and they get it, then you take them over there and they don't get it. You might need to repeat the activity in at least five different locations before the horse understands and it can be the same with the kids. That's helped me because now I don't get caught up in the emotion of the behaviour. I get caught up in: why is that kid behaving like that, what is it I don't understand, what is it I need to do differently to break it down further? You can't teach a kid or an animal when they're in stress.'

Jill began learning horsemanship skills at the age of thirty-two, when she got her first Thoroughbred. He was a really difficult horse and she wanted to understand him better. But she says she doesn't go for labelling horses (or people) with personality types.

'He was confused. My instruction was confused. My focus was confused. And he was stimulated by his environment more so than most horses. That was the problem.'

That horse, Deful, is now twenty-eight and still lives with Jill on her property. She credits him with being the first horse that took her down the path of learning to understand challenging behaviour.

'I learned an awful lot from that horse. He put me in hospital twice. He taught me never to take anything for granted with a horse. He's so very sensitive and reactive and driven by his environment.' Her students are often the same. 'They are driven externally by so many things.' Part of Jill's aim for working with those kids is to help them connect to what's driving them internally.

'It's trial and error. It's very intuitive. I read a lot of body language. I will pick up bits and pieces and I'll have my universal toolbox and I'll go into that toolbox and see what works for that particular individual at that particular time. I have enough confidence in myself now to know that if one tool isn't working, I don't need to panic, I just try something else. I do that with the kids and I'm starting to do that better with the horses.'

In the afternoon, an eight-year-old boy (we'll call him Sean) arrives with his mother. It's his second session and his hands and nose are pressed to the passenger-side window of the car, a massive grin on his face, his excited squeals audible through the glass.

His enthusiasm is a good sign, especially since he spent the whole of the first session disengaged and sulky.

He bounds over to us. His mother touches Elf's mane.

'Is this the pony that was dragged by the car?'

She goes on to tell me that Sean has high-functioning autism and ADHD. He's been excluded from mainstream school because 'he has a lot of problems communicating with children his own age and a lot of anxiety. He might push someone over just from that anxiety.'

And although this is only Sean's second session, he has told his mother that 'he feels like he knows what animals are thinking and they know what he's thinking'.

Sean is one of four children. 'For Sean to have this just for him makes him feel really good,' his mother says.

In today's session, Sean is focused, listening, calm. He and Elf make their way through multiple tasks. He grooms Elf and effectively tells the pony he's not allowed to eat grass while they're in the round yard. He leads him confidently and follows Jill's instructions to stop with the lead rope held to his belly to show

Elf to stop too. One of Jill's volunteers brings orange cones and a large hoop into the yard and Sean leads Elf around the cones and into the hoop and gets him to stop with all four hooves inside the hoop. Then Jill holds the hoop up on its edge and Sean thinks his way through the process of how to get both him and Elf to step through. Finally, a slightly more challenging task, he sends Elf through the hoop alone.

Sean has surpassed everyone's expectations. He's listened and followed instructions so well that Jill invites him to think about whether or not he would like to get up on a different horse after a few more lessons on the ground. Sean nods quickly, his eyes wide behind thick-lensed glasses.

The session concludes by leading Elf back into his roped-off area next to the stables in time for dinner. Jill invites Sean to help her feed him, and they carry the bucket of soaking hay to him and put it on the ground. Here is an opportunity to stimulate more senses. She invites him to smell the hay and taste the sugary water. To chew on a piece of soaked lucerne as though it was chewing gum. A fresh load of sawdust was delivered that morning and its piercing damp pine smell now floods the air all around the stables. They pat Elf some more and play with his mane.

Jill asks him how he feels when he's with Elf.

'Calm and slow.'

'Do you feel like that at school?' Jill asks, patting Elf at the same time.

Sean shakes his head.

'Now you just need to learn to take that feeling and carry it with you into your life at school,' Jill says. She spies the painting that Elf did earlier that day. 'Would you like to take this home with you? You could put it in your room and it can remind you of Elf.' Sean eagerly reaches for the painting. Then Jill reaches for a bot fly knife out of the grooming kit and cuts off a piece of Elf's mane and hands it to Sean. 'There you go. Now you can put that in your pocket and have a piece of Elf with you everywhere you go. Whenever you feel overwhelmed, you can just touch his mane and remember how you feel when you're with him.'

It's a moving end to what has been a clearly powerful session.

Late that afternoon, with the long shadows of the winter evening sending their icy fingers across the paddocks, Jill closes a gate and takes a long breath in.

'I'm still buzzing from that session,' she says, her eyes focused somewhere in the distance, her mind working, ticking, piecing bits of the puzzle together, already planning what she can do next to take Sean to a new level, analysing what she can take from that session and apply to other sessions. Then her thoughts turn to the war veterans coming for sessions soon and how she can start gathering research data on the effectiveness of her methods. There is no limit to her imagination.

'There's so far we can go with this. Who knows how many people we can help?'

And with Elf as her mascot, that reach stretches further every day. She's achieving what she's always wanted, one student at a time.

'I want people to think of Elf the pony and know that he is a symbol of hope for traumatised young people. That's what I want.'

GROOVER

The first time I speak with Australian Olympian Rebel Morrow, she is flustered, raw emotions bubbling to the surface every few seconds, her voice wavering and swaying. She drops her phone in the mud and apologises while she wipes it clean.

'I'm getting him back today,' she says, her words barely audible. 'He's coming home.' Her beloved horse, Groover, has just been cremated and his ashes are being delivered back to her in a box. 'He was only nineteen, not old. His life was too short.'

Rebel has an appearance to make at a dressage festival, where she is to deliver an inspiring speech about her and Groover's journey, which took her from saving him from death at the knackery all the way to the Athens Olympics. It's a story she's shared often but today she's hesitant.

'It's an emotional story at the best of times. I'm really not sure how I'm going to get through it now that he's gone.'

We decide to meet up again in a few weeks' time when her grief is not so overwhelming. In the end, Rebel felt unable to complete her speaking engagement and it takes another six months for her to be able to really talk with me about her life with Groover. He is written not only across her heart, but also across her skin in a tattoo dedicated to him on the inside of her left wrist, the Olympic rings on the inside of her right.

Rebel loved the small cattle town of Kilcoy in south-eastern Queensland where she grew up.

'My dad was a foreman at the Kilcoy Pastoral Company and a part-time farrier, and my mum was a professional western pleasure rider. I started in western pleasure and then moved into eventing. Kilcoy's such a great place. We rode horses up the road, I'd run and ride my bike around the town. The whole community knew us and if someone's kid was doing well, the community knew about it. And when the Olympics happened it took nothing for the whole town to get behind me and put *Go Rebel!* signs in the windows. So many people got so much out of me going there, not just myself and my family.'

Rebel says she didn't feel pressure from the town, only support.

'At that age, being twenty-seven, there was no weight of expectation. I was totally in the zone, totally loving it, totally over the moon, self-confident. There was no reason to doubt anything. This was my life and this was how it was. I never felt that there was ever going to be any outcome other than success. Now that I'm older, I need to do well because I need an income. But in my twenties? Nope. You get knocked down and you get back up again. As you get older, knocks have more impact. I just wanted to do a good job. But I didn't feel pressure from anyone.

'Actually, I didn't really even know how much was going on in Kilcoy at the time. It was only when I'd ring home and people would say, "Oh, you're in the papers again." Whereas, today, if you're competing, you still have constant contact via your mobile phone and social media and I think that could be distracting. But for me back then, I'd only just started emailing! The internet was a still a big deal. I wasn't exposed to all of that.'

Rebel has recently made the decision to downscale to five acres and focus on just a couple of her own horses, while maintaining a professional role in coaching riders and training horses. Her property has everything you'd expect of a competitor at her level: a dressage arena, grass paddocks, undercover yards with sawdust, jump-wings leaning against the fence, a shed the size of a small house and an enormous horse transport truck – all telling signs of just how serious a lifestyle this is for her.

Her two horses wander around, a young Warmblood–Thoroughbred cross named Adam, and her current star mount, Enny. Both of them are big, impressive chestnuts, just like Groover was.

'I don't go looking for chestnuts; they just seem to come to me.'

Rebel currently competes on Hillgrove Enviable (Enny – a Thoroughbred mare with the same sire as Groover), also a horse that came straight off the track.

'She's definitely the real McCoy in the Thoroughbred line. She's a hot mare and it takes a lot more tact with riding those horses. I was really fortunate with Groover. He was just such a simple, simple horse. What I achieved on him at that young age in my life was great, but who knows, if I'd had the mare I have now back then, who knows if I could have ridden her then like I can now with ten more years of experience.

'If a chance to go to the Olympics came my way again I wouldn't knock it back, that's for sure, but with horses it's such a process. You've got to have that horse for years and you've got to compete well for years, then it all goes on your record and you get selected off your record, and then within the three months out from an Olympic Games, if you don't do well then that's it. You could have campaigned amazingly in the last three years but if you don't do well in the last three months you're out. I'd love to say I'd do it again but it's just a massive process. Massive.

'This mare I have now definitely has the ability but I'm now that bit older and back then there was no real thought of how to survive life, I was just living the moment. I only own half of this mare so a decision will have to be made at some point whether I keep campaigning her or she gets sold to interested parties.'

Competitive riders frequently shy away from straight Thoroughbred horses, preferring something along the lines of a Warmblood, but Rebel has now ended up with two talented Thoroughbreds off the track.

'A Warmblood is the ideal horse for eventing because of the Warmblood movement and their temperament. But then you want the stamina of the Thoroughbred to last the three days of a competition. When I grew up, a Thoroughbred was all we were able to have, there were so many of them around, so I just have an ability to ride that type of horse. I do seem to just click with the Thoroughbreds more.

'I love working with horses that have come off the track.

There's such a deep sense of satisfaction in getting a horse working well and giving it a second chance. But I don't take on any more of them now. It's my new thing because I can't rescue them all, I can't make them all better and I can't rehome them all. And they're not all going to be good, that's for sure. All the rest can't make the grade because they're either physically unsound or mentally damaged. And they just don't have the same talent. I can't save them all so I don't even want to look at them. I just don't want to be tempted by them any more. There are just too many. There might be other rescue horses out there that have gone far in competitions, but not to the Olympics. I was just lucky with Groover.'

Groover entered Rebel's life when she was twenty. Wanting to work with and ride horses professionally, she made the pragmatic decision after school to take on hard physical work at the Kilcoy meatworks for four years to save enough money to fund her equine dreams.

'It was just a means to an end. Back then it was such a family-oriented business, so they were very accommodating with the times I worked and the times I needed off to go and ride. The company was very good to me. I can't say I enjoyed working there but it was good money and you need money to fund horses. It was just a period in my life.'

There is one lingering effect of her time there, though. 'I'm not a vegetarian but I don't eat red meat, just from the smell of the meatworks. I like eating duck, but I think about the duck while I'm eating it. I accept that's the way of life.'

It was during this time that she met Oaklea Groover.

'My dad had a professional relationship with the master farrier Craig Jones, and Craig's wife, Jenny Jones, was doing track work. Groover was one of the horses she used to ride. He was only four and had been no good as a racehorse. The owners gave him to me to trial him for a month because they wanted to try him back at racing after that. He was well bred and showed promise but he just didn't have that killer instinct in him. So I tried him and he was amazing, straight up.'

Rebel had one other horse at the time, a mare called Oaklea Reprieve (Tammy), who was also very talented and placing at high levels of competition. Initially, Tammy was Rebel's mother's western pleasure horse but Rebel says she quickly 'stole' her when she showed signs of 'brilliance', and went on to place fifth at the Sydney Olympic selection event in 2004. In an ideal world, a competitive rider would have more than one horse to work with, given the amount of time it takes to develop them and the risks involved of something happening to that one horse. So Rebel was open to the idea of taking on another.

'I was jumping Groover one day and I said to Mum, "You know, if I was ever to go to the Olympics, this would be the horse I would go on." Before that, I don't think I'd ever said it out loud. But he was different. Completely different to anything else I'd ever ridden. I'd never felt that sort of jump in a Thoroughbred. Yes, I've felt an amazing jump in an expensively bred horse because they should feel like that if that's what you've spent money on.

'I'd taken him to a show at Mt Gravatt and I was competing on other horses at that show and I had Groover on trial. I took him down, not to compete, but just to see what he was like out in the open. You don't just hop on an ex-racehorse and take them to an event. But I did and at the end of the day I took him and jumped over some of the jumps and I remember how my face was just ecstatic and I was smiling the whole time. For him to do what he'd just done when I'd only had him for a couple of weeks . . . something was so different with him.'

It was an illuminating moment that gave Rebel a certainty in her bones that would keep her going through the horrific surgeries to come, and keep her faith in their partnership. For this journey to the Olympics wasn't to be an easy fairy tale.

'He started to get this discharge out of his nose. It was this bloody yellowy serum that would come out. He loved to roll in the dirt and we thought maybe he'd hit his head. We told the owners when he was due to go back to the track and they took him to the vet's. Then we heard what he had.'

Groover was diagnosed with ethmoid haematomas, a debilitating, progressive and chronic condition in which bloody haematomas grow in the sinus cavities of the nose and skull, causing bleeding, respiratory issues and other degeneration of tissues in the head.

'You have to treat them or put the horse down because they just end up getting bigger and bigger and they'll just haemorrhage.'

Groover's racing owners decided not to treat him and planned instead to send him to the knackery. Rebel bought him for three hundred dollars, the price the owners would have got for him as his value in meat weight.

That initial payment quickly escalated with the treatments and surgery, which Rebel estimates cost somewhere between fifteen and twenty thousand dollars.

'The first vet drilled a hole in his skull and injected formalin into his head to eat away the haematoma. That was the first thing to try, to see if it would help. It killed some of it, but then the haematoma went further up into his skull to try to move away from the formalin, and then it eventually moved across to the other side of his skull and filled that up as well.

'By that time, I'd moved from Kilcoy down to New South Wales and he'd come with me because he was still healthy and happy and I was competing on him and he'd got up to pre-novice level. That's when I took him to a surgeon in Sydney, who was the man of the moment for any kind of difficult surgeries. He had to open up his skull, totally take off flaps. Groover got such a bumpy head because he had so many surgeries.'

In photographs of the handsome chestnut, it is easy to see the lumps on either side of the midline of his forehead, above each eye.

'So they opened up one side and took it all out and then they put the flaps back on and stapled his skull back together. He had to go back in and get the other side opened to take it out of there. The surgeries were a year apart because each one was such a massive operation, they couldn't do it all at once. After each one, he'd have a couple of months off. I could still walk and trot on him and it kept his nasal passages blowing all the time. All this disgusting muck from his head would come out after what they'd done in the surgery.'

Complications followed, though, and Groover suffered a serious infection after the second operation.

'At that point, the vet said he couldn't promise me that it would ever stop coming back. He said I'd have to make a decision on whether to keep putting Groover through this or to put him down. It was just such a hard decision to make. He was probably only one-star level then, but everything else about him was 100 per cent sound and great. He was such an amazing horse but he just had this trauma in his head the whole time. I couldn't make that decision to put him down so we went ahead with more treatments and the infection cleared up.'

Luckily it was a turning point, and from then on he went forward in leaps and bounds. 'He never fully recovered from it, though. I had to keep getting him checked all the time, every six months, then out to a year. After that big infection in his head he only had a couple more treatments where they just stuck a scope up his nose to dab the formalin in different places at different times. They never opened his head again after that, which was a relief because it was such a terrible thing.

'The vet said Groover was such a strong horse and must be destined for something great because they just didn't survive that many surgeries and losing that much blood each time.'

The vet wasn't alone in that sense of destiny. It was the same feeling Rebel had had when she first rode him over those jumps. The same feeling that made her voice that daring prediction that Groover would be the horse she would go to the Olympics with.

'Growing up, I always spoke about going to the Olymics, but as a runner. I loved running and did a lot of athletics at school but I only ever got as far as the state titles and then they'd run rings around me. I trained hard and I wanted to progress but every time I got to the state titles they would beat me. So that dream was starting to diminish and by Year 12 I'd stopped because if I couldn't win then I didn't want to do it. I always rode but I never thought of going to the Olympics that way.

'After I finished school, I kept riding and kept competing but it wasn't until I rode Groover and he jumped those few jumps that I declared to Mum that he was going to take me there.'

Even then, Rebel says it didn't become her single focus. She knew she wanted to ride professionally, but the journey to the Olympics was still a bit more accidental than that.

'I just started getting better, and winning, and understanding riding more and understanding horses more. As a kid I would just ride and I would win but it was only because I was a good rider. It was probably when Groover reached a two-star level (the fifth of seven levels, with four-star being the world competition level) and I overheard some of the equestrian greats start to make comments about how good Groover was, that the initial hope I'd had with Groover when I first rode him started to really sink in as reality.

'He did it all. There wasn't anything he didn't like. He did it all so easily. Nothing was hard for him.'

Rebel says it's a completely different story with her current horse, Enny.

'She doesn't enjoy the dressage. She can do it easily but she stresses and suffers from anxiety. I don't know if she loves performing. Groover did. I could feel that in him. He would go out on show. He'd move from the warm-up area to the arena and I could feel him inflate, whereas Enny tightens up and is happy when it's over. He was a total all-rounder, loved every phase. He didn't have a weakness. I would have been his weakness with my lack of experience and my lack of confidence and my nerves at that age. He was a bit slow, that's all. I had to kick him, *a lot*, to make him go fast. He was never in a hurry.'

When Rebel chose to save Groover from the knackery it was because she'd found that special once-in-a-lifetime connection and had seen the huge potential in him that others hadn't seen.

'I'd already fallen for him. But if I was put in that same situation again, with a horse needing that kind of surgery, and the horse didn't have Groover's ability and his amazing personality, I wouldn't go through it again – financially or emotionally, or putting the horse through it. The humane thing is to put them down. It was quite horrific.'

Groover's lovely nature also won over Rebel's heart, though she admits he wasn't perfect.

'He kicked me once and detached my nose from my face. He and another horse were having a bit of a stand-off while Groover was tied up. He was gelded late in life so he still had a few stallion ways about him. I was putting his work boots on and I'd gone around the other side of him and he just double-barrelled me. I got thrown backwards. Mum and Dad were there and Mum looked over at me and went white. I looked at her and said, "What's wrong?" and at the same time I could feel that my shirt was getting hot. I looked down and there was blood all over it. The end of his shoe had just cut straight through the bottom of my nose and my lip had dropped. I had to go to hospital, and twenty stitches later my nose was back on my face. He wasn't deliberately aiming at me but he was so focused on being manly with the other horse he just reacted. I didn't hold a grudge against him. I adored him and I just thought it was an accident.'

For anyone to be chosen for the Australian Olympic team they will have dedicated years of their life, suffered and recovered from injuries, devoted their focus and energy and likely have spent a lot of their personal money along the way. In this sense, Rebel is no different. But as an equestrian, she also has the additional (hefty) expenses of caring for a horse, the constant and lengthy on-road travel around the country to compete (time for which she doesn't get paid) and the additional worry that the horse will be fit and healthy enough to withstand competition. Both she and the horse need to have the competitive capacity at the same time. A lot of stars need to align in order for both horse and rider to make it. It's a unique and rare combination. Add to that the extreme surgeries Groover went through in his life and you've got something close to a miracle.

'So much of it comes down to a lot of bloody luck. I won that event selection in Sydney for the team to go to Athens. But at the third-last fence in cross-country, coming down the hill, Groover was a bit tired, I was a bit tired, and he hit his knee on the jump. And we nearly toppled over. I was holding onto his neck for five strides before I got back on and finished it. But if I'd fallen off? I wouldn't have gone to the Olympics. There's a massive amount of luck in the end of it all as well.'

Equestrian competitors are chosen as a partnership with their horse. If anything happens to either rider or their nominated mount, that ends the journey.

'Look at the last Olympics. One of the Australian team's horses went unsound while over there, and then the reserve horse got a hoof abscess. You can be there, on site, and it can still go wrong.'

Fortunately, Rebel and Groover's lead-up to, and participation in, the games went smoothly.

'The team vet visited the horses often and flew around to wherever they were to make sure they were all still healthy and good to go. Then the horses stayed in Sydney for a week to make sure they were okay. From there, they flew straight to England and we stayed there for a month before the Olympics because you have to have time for them to recover, and if they get travel sickness they need to recover from that, and they have to adjust to the opposite season. Fortunately, none of them got sick. Next, the flight to Athens was only an hour and half. Then after their events were done, they were flown straight back to England and started their quarantine the next day, which is a good month in a special area. I stayed there the whole time. Finally they flew back to Sydney and they went to quarantine in Eastern Creek for another week.

'I drove to see him whenever I could but over that whole two-month period he was out of my care for most of the time and I was relying on other people to look after him. It was hard. Up until that point, from the moment I got Groover he'd been in my day-to-day care. He was okay in the sense that he was such an easy, easy horse. He was not a special needs horse. I had no worries with that. I wasn't stressed about him on the plane because he wasn't a stressed horse. I knew he wouldn't go ballistic with the noise or the motion or anything. They travel with some vets and some grooms on cargo planes. They get their own stalls but they can't walk around in their stalls or lie down.

'Whatever their dietary needs are, you just tell them and they organise it for you. Groover was simple to feed. He ate a lot of grain because he was a really laidback horse. He was on six kilos a day of a formula designed for turbo racehorses! The mare I ride now, who is by the same sire, gets nothing. She wouldn't even know what one of those bags looks like! Even though Groover was extremely powerful and sensational in that way, Enny's just got a bigger motor that goes from nought to a hundred really fast. She's faster than Groover ever was.'

He may have been slow, but Groover performed well in Athens.

'We were coming seventh after the dressage event, which is a huge field, and I have to remember that it's the best competitors in the world, so seventh in the world feels pretty good. He did his usual good test but then in the rein back, where you halt and walk back, he threw his head up, which he'd never, ever done and it was really bizarre. So we didn't get a good mark for that one but the rest was really good. I will never forget that feeling. I'll never forget the silence of being in the arena and doing it. I could hear his breathing, and my breathing, and his footfalls. That silence is amazing.

'Cross-country was after that. He got a two-second time penalty but the whole round was sensational. I can remember seeing Dad on one of the corners, behind the bunting. You wouldn't think you could see anyone but as I went around this corner I could see this man standing there and waving his flag. I could hear, "Go, Rebel!" And that came out, above everything else in the crowd. And Dad had brought this hat with "100 per cent Rebel" on it and I could see that. I kept looking at him as I went round the corner. It was amazing. There was only one scary moment over a jump but Groover fixed himself up and we went well.'

The final round of the three-day event is showjumping.

'I really suffered with nerves. I was nervous in all three rounds but I really struggled in the showjumping, which was normal for me at that time. Now that I'm a bit older I'm better with it. It's still my weakest phase, but I'm more confident in it now than I was back then. He was great in that round. He had a rail down in the first round and made it into the next round to jump-off with the highest scorers for an individual medal. We came eleventh individually and the Australian team came sixth overall.'

Most people would consider that result to be wonderful but Rebel wishes it were different.

'It was a shame. I felt it. All the other years, Australia had won gold, and it was a real shame for me personally. Now I get even more disappointed because I haven't been again and who knows if I'll go again, so the competitor in me is disappointed. But hopefully – hopefully! – I'll get to do it again.'

Rebel has deep appreciation of the strong partnership she shared with Groover and the legacy he has left her.

'I got away with a lot with Groover and I was fortunate to have him at that stage in my life. I definitely couldn't have coped with Enny in my twenties. She's hard to manage. She's very talented. She's got the goods to go to the Olympics and the World Games. I keep going with her because she's all I've got. She's my horse and I can manage. I don't have five horses I can choose from or five owners who can pay to have another one better than Enny for me.

'Groover made people believe in fate and good luck. That partnership with Groover was so special for me but his story is just as special for the others who hear it. It gives them hope that they can achieve their dreams. And I was one of those people. I think we're all ordinary until we do something extraordinary and he enabled me to be that, to be a name people know, and to set myself up for life. It's a fantastic feeling to be good at something. When you're having a bad day you can still rely on that and now I've got that security for the rest of my life.

'But we only got to enjoy being great for such a short time. We'd done all the hard yards and he didn't have to be trained any more in that sense; there were no more hard training sessions to be done.'

Groover suffered a bad injury to his sacroiliac joint in his hips just before he and Rebel were due to go to Aachen, Germany, for the World Games after the Olympics, so they couldn't attend. A year later, he'd recovered from that injury but then fractured his femur at home, alone in the paddock, which was the end of his competitive career.

He retired on Rebel's parents' property in New South Wales where he spent many years being loved and pampered. Sadly, in 2013, a tendon injury, which was too severe to be treated, ended his young life.

'Groover's story gives "normal" people such hope. I had a talent, for sure, but I was normal – until Groover came along. He brought out the best in me and I brought out the best in him. That's why his story touches people. It's like if someone wins the lottery and you hear that story, you think, *Well, maybe that could be me one day*. It's a one-in-a-zillion chance, but it's a chance. It's the same as getting that horse off the track and going to the Olympics. That's a one-in-a-million chance. You need to have the skills and the access to everything you need to achieve that.'

Despite Rebel's protests that she won't take on any ex-racehorses again, there is a small crack in her resolve.

'I think I need to take moments to appreciate what I've done. With Enny, four years ago she was just a wild ex-racehorse, and now I'm taking her to Adelaide to compete in a four-star event. And others in the field will be competing on a really flash horse and I'll be sitting there on this wild horse. In presentations, she's terrible. She hates standing. She hates the crowds. And when they clap she bolts on me. So I'm on the back foot. But I can still do it on the back foot. And to do it that way is just so rewarding and sensational.

'So, look, if the right horse came along again, yeah, maybe . . . But I'm *not* looking for it!'

SOUL

On the very day that a bay and white foal was to be sold and taken to a new home, he fell over a cliff and lay at the bottom, unmoving. That foal would be dead now if it wasn't for Beverly Finnigan.

'It was September 2011 and I was driving with a friend and my two daughters to go and look at a couple of nice young foals and yearlings we wanted to buy. We got halfway to the property and my phone rang. It was my husband and he said the man that owned the horses had just rung and said not to go up to the property as the young paint colt I was going to look at wasn't going to make it to the end of the day. He'd said the horse had fallen down a cliff and was going to be shot. I put my foot down, dropped my children off with my friend's husband, because I didn't want them to see the horse get shot, and we took off up to the property.

'Five minutes later, we found the property owner and asked what had happened. He said he didn't know but the horse was down a 20-metre embankment and he was just getting his rifle to go and shoot him. I asked if the horse had broken his legs or hurt himself badly but he just said he didn't know and wasn't climbing down to find out. So we went up the mountain with him to see if we could do anything for the young horse.

'We got to the very top of the ridge and got out of the car. By then, the other horses in the herd had left. Even the colt's own mother had gone, so we thought the worst. Surely his mother wouldn't give up without knowing there was no hope for him.

'We looked over the edge of the cliff but couldn't see a thing, let alone a horse. The owner told us to walk down the cliff a bit and we'd see him. So we slid down a little, hanging onto shrubs and weeds so we didn't fall too far. Then three quarters of the way down this very steep ridge we could see the bay and white colours of the colt. He was lying in a really bad position, with his legs up the cliff and his back wedged by the stump of a small tree. He was lying in bracken fern and bits of weed. So we set down the cliff to see if we could get a better look at him. When we got near him, we could see it was his wither (the high point at the top of the shoulders) that was the only thing stopping him from ending up further down the cliff. It was wedged into the tree stump.

'These horses had never been handled. They'd never had their feet or teeth done, or been wormed. They'd never seen their mothers being touched so we were expecting the worst. We were sure if we went near this horse he would explode with fear.

'But it was the most amazing thing. He just lay there, not moving, not trying to get up to get away from us. We put it down to shock and sheer exhaustion from his ordeal. Of course, we couldn't leave the poor little horse like that.

'Very gently, we came closer and felt his legs, stretched them out and checked for breaks. There was nothing – he seemed injury-free, which was unbelievable, considering his fall. So of course we said we would do whatever we could to help him. He didn't deserve to be shot.'

What followed was a long, stressful and strenuous exercise to try and rescue Soul. Beverly and her friend climbed back up the cliff and began phoning anyone and everyone who might be able to help. She and the property owner went back to his house to get his tractor and search for something they could use as a sling. Horse rescue of this nature is fraught with danger to both the people and the horse. Many attempts such as these end in tragedy, because either the incorrect rescue slings and ropes are used or they are applied to the most vulnerable parts of the horse, such as the legs, tail or head and neck. Fortunately for Soul, Beverly managed to find some cow slings that could be improvised to ensure they were broad enough and safe enough to not hurt Soul. They also took chains and ropes and a bucket of water, hoping to stave off the dehydration he was likely experiencing.

'Down the cliff we went again. We put a halter and lead on him to see if we could pull his head up a little to get him off his wither and also so he didn't bloat from facing downhill for so long. His tummy was already full of gas and hard. His eyes had good colour though, so that gave us hope. We tried to get the sling around him but he was just too heavy for us. So we had to make more phone calls and get a few more big blokes out there. Finally, we got the sling under him. It took the tractor and all of us to be able to roll him over so that his back was facing uphill for the big drag up.'

Bev may have breathed a sigh of relief at this point, but it was far from over. It was a huge journey for Soul to be dragged up the cliff. Compounding the problems were larger trees in the path of where Soul had to be dragged.

'We attached smaller ropes onto the main rope and twisted them around other trees off to the side so that when the tractor pulled we could try to take the weight over to one side away from the tree that was in the road. It wasn't easy. We were exhausted. Adrenaline was the only thing keeping us going.

'We had one friend working Soul's halter lead so that his head wouldn't twist under himself. Eventually, we got him to the top of the mountain. We tried to drag him onto an even area, which wasn't easy as it was a ridgeline and on both sides were steep drops. We let him rest for quite some time, then made a phone call and ordered a tetanus vaccine from the vet. The property owner's wife drove to town and got that for us and we gave it to him as soon as she came back. We still couldn't believe we didn't have to sedate him at all to get him up. Not once did he throw his head, kick out or try to fight us in any way. He was an amazing young horse with more trust than any horse I've ever come across.

'We gave him a bucket of water, which he drank, and a biscuit of hay, which he set about eating.

'After an hour or so we had to try and get him on his feet. We'd just spent five hours trying to save him and we still had no idea if he was going to make it. Everyone was saying the same thing, that there was no way he could have gotten out of that without at least one major injury. We all got around him and tried to lift him to his feet but he wouldn't even try. No matter what we did he wouldn't get up. At that point, I thought it was over. I thought the worst, that he must have had major spinal injuries and we'd have to put him down. It was devastating after all the effort. And we'd all become very attached to Soul in that short time.'

Bev has tears in her eyes remembering that day.

'The property owner suggested we try to lift him with the tractor bucket, as you do with cows if they go down. So we gave it a go. We lifted him enough that his feet touched the ground and even then he didn't try to stand or walk or fight. He just hung there in the sling. It was such a sad moment.

'But we kept trying. We massaged his legs again and stretched them. We tried everything. He couldn't be left on the ridge; he'd end up back down the cliff on his own.

'We carefully drove the tractor down the ridge, holding Soul's head up for him. He didn't mind that I was under him holding his chin in the air so it didn't hang. We went right down the ridge with him free-swinging in the sling till we got down near his mate, a Shetland pony. We started to lower the bucket on the tractor so that he could feel the ground under his feet and finally he started to scramble for ground. We were so happy.

'Very gently, we lowered him and let him stand for ten minutes before taking off all of his ropes and belts. And there he was – on the ground, with all four feet standing on his own. We couldn't have been happier.

'He tentatively walked off, very stiff and with a bit of a limp on his front left leg. And then he started to eat. He was such a tough little horse.'

Bev knew for sure there was no way she was leaving Soul there. She told the owner she'd let him rest for a few days and then come back and pick him up. But the very next day, the owner rang to say that Soul had 'gotten into strife again'. He'd gone for a drink at the back of the property and become bogged in the mud. No doubt he was still very weak and tired from his ordeal the day before.

'By the time I got there they had him out of the dam. The owner said he had to be dragged a good hundred meters to safety before he could let him go again. I'm not sure the dragging would have been very pleasant as I'm pretty sure the owner didn't use the slings we'd made but rather just pulled him out by the neck.'

Understandably, Bev decided to collect Soul as soon as possible. She went back the next day and, despite Soul's first experiences with humans being nothing but traumatic, he walked up the cattle ramp like he'd done it a thousand times and stood stock still all the way home on the truck.

'When we got him home, we lowered the tailgate and I put his lead on his halter and he walked off the truck with me like a pro. I put him in yards, fed and watered him, and cleaned up his wounds. The next day I wormed him. He was a little lethargic for twenty-four hours until all of his worms let go. I have never seen so many worms in a horse in my life. He had two worming treatments and put on good weight in just ten days. Then I put him in his own little yard full of grass up at the house and I bathed him, which he loved, and he just got better every day.'

Soul had been through an incredible ordeal and had been rescued and given the chance of a whole new life. He stayed with Bev for a year and then he was given the chance to pay it forward and change someone else's life.

Kelsie Consadine has been around horses her whole life.

'My grandfather was a trainer of racehorses and my dad

started riding at twelve. He became a jockey for my grandfather and rode his first race at sixteen. My pop was training and my dad was riding the racehorses in training and racing on the weekend. Dad grew out of that jockey lifestyle, though. It's very hectic, really hard on the system. So then he became a trainer and focused more on the horse breaking and training side of it.

'By the time I came around in 1994 my dad was a licensed trainer. He worked at our local racetrack and I used to go to work with him every morning at three a.m. He'd pull me out of bed and put me in the back seat of the car where he'd made up a little bed and I'd sleep there until sunrise. Then I'd get up and walk down to the stables and sit on the fences and watch the horses go round. I have done bits and pieces of track work for other people but seeing how many damaging falls my dad had – he's in his forties now and he's practically crippled – I decided to steer away from it. It's not really my cup of tea.'

Kelsie's dad manages a stud near Allora in Queensland, while Kelsie lives with her mother in Grafton, New South Wales. They live on a suburban block but have access to property on the outskirts of town where they keep their horses and cattle.

Kelsie has two horses of her own, Soul and Little Bear. Soul came first and was a highly considered addition to Kelsie's life after years of effort on her part to get herself well.

'I was really lost. I know most teens don't really have a sense of direction but I was truly lost. I had no idea why I was waking up every day. Everything was just routine to me, as though my body did it without thinking or feeling and I felt very distant.'

Kelsie was suffering with mental illness.

'I have non-melancholic unipolar disorder. Being a unipolar

depression means it's made up of very long lows. There's a big history of mental illness in the family, including suicidal tendencies in the past. I was told that my condition is sort of genetic. I lived with my father for a while when I was fourteen and it just didn't work out. I was a teenage girl and wanted my privacy and my dad didn't understand that and I started really rebelling in school. I started experiencing panic attacks, insomnia. I was paranoid all the time that someone was watching me or was going to say something to me and thinking badly of me all the time. I was constantly apologising for even existing. I'd ask stupid questions.'

But the road to diagnosis was a long and difficult one.

'Because I was fifteen, and that's the age when the hormones really kick in, it was very hard for me to get a diagnosis and get looked at. I would just sleep all day. I wouldn't come out of my room. Nothing brought me enjoyment, nothing gave me that little spark. I was just empty. It took quite a long time to get doctors to actually look at it and consider it as something serious because they said it was just hormones and I'd just get over it in time. It wasn't until I went through a lot of bullying – I would get into a serious fight with someone and then I'd self-harm as a way of releasing that tension and panic – that they started to reconsider their opinion. That's when I went to a psychologist and a psychiatrist and that's the diagnosis they came back with.

'It was definitely very hard because I was so young and the medications hadn't really been tested on people that young, so they were very particular about giving me medication.'

Kelsie followed their recommended treatment path for a long time.

'For quite some time I saw three different professionals and

I went onto medication and then I did a lot of cognitive behavioural therapy, where they encourage the positive behaviour to create the chain of positive wellbeing. So, the theory goes that you choose something you know you used to enjoy and do it. And even though you may not enjoy it at the start, if you keep going, eventually you'll come back into sync with it. For me, that activity was horses.

'But then the medication stopped working and they put me onto another one and I started to experience feelings said to be like speed. I was very up and down. I had teachers in class calling my mum, very worried because I'd be over the top, wouldn't be able to stop talking, and then next thing I'd be an absolute mess. So in the end, after trying all these different medications I called it quits. I said I wouldn't take any more medication, that I would fix the problem myself, in a more natural way.

'I weaned myself off them over a couple of weeks and there were a lot of head spins and headaches but I wanted to feel feelings that were normal for me. I didn't want to live any more in the frame of feelings those drugs were creating. They made me feel happy and lightheaded and as though everything was hunky-dory but I didn't want to do that any more. I wanted real things that would make me really happy – authentic happiness.'

That took Kelsie on the search for a young horse to start under saddle herself.

'I'd been looking for ages. They were way too expensive. I kept getting offered all these pedigree bloodlines, bred to do this and bred to do that, two thousand dollars each. I started to give up. I thought it was ridiculous. Surely there was someone out there who had a little horse that someone else could take on. Then

I posted a note on a group in Facebook and said I wanted an unbroken horse under five hundred dollars. And that was when Bev popped up and said, "I have the horse for you."

'Soul was located in Doubtful Creek, in between Casino and Kyogle, around an hour and a half from my home. As soon as she said she had a brilliant little paint horse that was a real girl's horse, and she only wanted four hundred dollars for him, everyone jumped onto the Facebook post saying they wanted him. So we deleted the post and she emailed me photos. Bev didn't even have him up for sale; it was only that she saw my ad and decided that maybe it was time to let him move on to someone else because she didn't have the time for him. She emailed me tonnes of pictures of him, and we talked via email every day.'

'I'm not sure what made me respond to Kelsie's advert,' Bev says. 'I read Kelsie's ad and thought I'd contact her. I didn't have Soul for sale and I was happy for him to spend his days out in the paddock for as long as he needed. But after emailing Kelsie a few times, and having a lot of other people trying to buy Soul out from under her, I just liked her. There was something about her that made it feel right. I sold Soul for four hundred and that was only to recover some of the major costs. I'd had him gelded and his feet had been an ongoing expense that I knew Kelsie would have to continue with. I like helping people out as well and I think I thought this horse, no matter how bad a start he had, he was going to turn into the perfect horse for Kelsie.'

Kelsie says it took Bev a long time to open up and tell her what had really happened to Soul.

'I think she was scared that once she told me I'd run for the hills. But something in Soul's story sparked something in me. It was that idea of him being hauled up from the cliff in the jaws of life. That's what I wanted for me: something to pull me out of the deep hole of misery and uncertainty I was in. Here stood a little horse that never asked for his fate of nearly being destroyed, and there I was, creating my own fate, being so selfish and wanting to end it all. If anything, he became an inspiration to me. He needed someone to take over leading him down the path of life, and I needed some form of existence and purpose to understand the sort of distance I felt. I knew that together we could bring each other back to the land of the living.

'She told me that he came with a name but if I didn't like it I could change it. She said, "His name's Soul because he's like an old soul. It's like he's been here before." And then when she told me his story I thought there was no way I was going to change that. We call him Old Soul because he just took everything that happened to him in his stride. I don't know what made Bev keep driving that day. I don't know if she even knows to this day, but she kept going.

'She had him for about a year before she sold him to me. He was very worm-infested and so Bev had done a lot of handling with him, catching him and worming him and treating his external injuries. And she'd had to do a lot with his feet, too; they'd been in such wet country they'd caved in, and they're only just coming good now. Because of the accident he was so emotionally shut-down that he'd become a very one-person horse. He didn't accept anyone else. Bev was his lady and that was it. He was very wary of anyone else.'

Kelsie first saw Soul in September 2012. 'I was on my way back from a rodeo in Warwick and I'd organised with Bev to have a look at him on the way home. I had a fifty-dollar deposit ready. When I turned up, Bev had him in the driveway and he was the cutest little thing I'd ever seen. He was all fluffy, he had a big pod gut. He had big donkey ears and this little head. And as soon as I saw him, I thought, *Oh my God*. Bev started saying how he was very wary after the accident and you had to really take your time and wait until he accepted you as number one. And I suppose, looking back on myself and everything I was going through at the time, I wasn't very trusting and the only person I ever confided in was my mother. I found myself very distant from everyone else. I lost a lot of friends because I didn't really have the will to communicate. So I guess I knew where Soul was coming from.

'He wouldn't let me touch him for the first ten minutes. It was a merry-go-round and I chased him around in a circle. But once I got my hand on his neck and he realised I wasn't going to eat him, that was it. After that he came up and leaned right on me for a scratch. He was sniffing me and nibbling on my hair. He was picking grass up and sprinkling it over me. I knew that he was desperate to be that sort of horse but you could just tell by his body language and the way he stood that he just wasn't sure. It took a long time for him to even act like a horse and run around and buck and eat out of a bucket. I returned at the end of that month with a horse float and the rest of the money and took him home.

'The morning I went to pick him up I was just a kid at Christmas. I've never felt excitement like that. It was so overwhelming and I kept getting nauseous on the way up and we had to keep stopping because my body was just so full of adrenaline. After I got him home I just wanted to spend every waking minute with him. I wanted to get out of bed, I wanted to have breakfast,

I wanted to get dressed, I wanted to go and see my horse.

'For a while I got a bit worried and thought I'd bitten off more than I could chew. This was a two-year-old horse that had very little handling and had no idea of respect for humans. The first day I had him in the yard he turned around and lunged at me and bit me. I knew that was him trying to assert dominance by saying, "Look what I'm capable of, please don't hurt me." So he got chastised for it but he didn't get completely roused on.

'Once all the excitement settled down I could feel myself building up. I used to hate socialising and going out and being with people. I'd keep thinking, *I just want to go home, I just want to go home, I just want to go home.* I felt like being around people or any sort of situation that required me to communicate was very overwhelming, so to wake up feeling positive and wanting to go out in the sunshine and wanting to see my horse and wanting to actually put effort into anything gave me hope. It came back steadily and surely, without me really having to try. When I came off the medication, I had to put in a lot of effort into convincing myself that it was going to be okay and I didn't need it. Whereas after I had Soul, it just came back really naturally and I could feel myself getting higher and higher.

'But because I was so involved with my own progress – feeling better, happier and more positive than I was before – I forgot that Soul was still dealing with his own problems. We went downhill there for a little bit because I thought, *well, I'm right, so Soul will be too*. But that wasn't the case. Because he wasn't working out as well as I hoped, it was bringing me back down. So I turned him out with an old gelding for three and a half months to grow and just be a horse, no pressure.

'During that time I felt lost. I wanted to bring him back in every day. But I could see the change in him, like the change in me. To start with, he just trotted up the hill and didn't want to be a part of daily feeding and visits. Then he came down the hill a little bit and just looked at me and then turned away and went back up the hill. Every day I could see him feeling better and better until he'd do a mad bolt down to the fence, bucking and carrying on. It was like a cycle. I could see Soul getting better, and then I could feel myself getting better. Then I could see him getting better again, and I felt better again. And slowly but surely, we helped each other out.

'He became a part of the herd. To begin with, he wouldn't lie down. The others would all lie down to sleep but he would keep standing. Now, he's got to the point where he'll be lying down in the sun having a sleep and won't get up until I'm right on top of him. He's come forward in leaps and bounds.

'At this stage, he's been mouthed [introduced to a metal bit in his mouth] and backed [had someone sit on him]. I can put a tarp over him. I can put a tarp over his head. You can crack a whip near him. I've ridden him. He's never put a foot wrong. He's been the most pleasant horse to break in. He was the first horse I broke in by myself. I grew up seeing my dad do it and I learned a lot from him but Soul was my first time by myself without any help. It's given me a lot of confidence, and I'm very proud to call him my horse. He's absolutely lovely and well put together.

'I do a lot of contract mustering so I'm hopefully turning him into one of our mustering mounts. Soul has wonderful bloodlines for being a really good cow horse and that's what drew Bev to him in the first place. I want to do as much as possible with him.

He has the potential to go so far in anything he does. He has this all-or-nothing spirit. I really want to campdraft [competitive cattle handling on horseback, where the rider moves a steer through an obstacle course] with him and educate him to barrel race. He's very good with cattle, even now.'

Life is looking up for Kelsie. 'I've started back at TAFE and I've just finished my Certificate II in horse industries. I'm doing my Certificate III in horse breeding now, then I go on to another level in equine nursing, so I'm hoping I can get somewhere in that industry. I definitely want to follow that path because of Soul. If it wasn't for all those people that day who helped pull him up that cliff, he wouldn't be here today at all. I'm very blessed.'

Soul clearly brings Kelsie the joy she was looking for, and so too does her second horse, Little Bear, also a rescue horse.

'I got him after I got Soul and his name is Little Bear because he's fat and fluffy and looks just like a little bear. He's a miniature. I bought him out of the dogger section of the local sales for forty dollars. He was a stallion when I got him and he had been abused because he will not tolerate men of any sort. He can't handle it. It's been a long road with him as well because he was very emotionally shut-down like Soul was, so he's just enjoying being a horse at the moment. He's a little ratbag, but he's a little character. He's the mischief-maker in the whole lot of them.'

While Kelsie is off medication and Soul has brought a lot of improvement into her life, it's not a total fix. She says it's still an up-and-down journey, but she now has more resources to help her deal with the downs.

'The coping mechanisms now are very different than they were before. Riding and working with the horse is my biggest frustration release. It's therapy. It's like going to gym and running ten kilometres on a treadmill. It's a release. It's healing.'

From Bev's perspective, she sees only great things in the relationship between Kelsie and the colt that fell of the cliff.

'When Kelsie came to look at Soul for the first time, he melted in her hands and her into him. Not once did she want to push him or ask anything of him other than to just stand with him. Sometimes animals and people just connect and this was one of those times. I knew he'd look after her and she'd look after him. She promised me she'd stay in touch and send me regular photos and she's kept her promise.

'Soul was named Soul because it was like he had been on this earth a lot longer than he had. He had an old soul. From what I've seen of Kelsie, and the way she speaks, I would say the same of her. They're perfect for each other.'

DALLAS

Olivia Ruzicka's best friend in the world is her horse, Dallas. Standing next to Olivia, he exudes a solid calmness that is warm and comforting. He oozes personality. She leads him to the cut of wood that serves as her mounting block and, unasked, he puts both feet up on it and stands there, looking around the gorgeous property where he is agisted, on the hills above the Tamar River in Launceston, Tasmania. Then he turns his head to her and she kisses him on the cheek and his big dark eyes close in relaxation.

When you talk with thirteen-year-old Olivia Ruzicka, you cannot help but smile. She is bright and bubbly and her enthusiasm for life and, especially, horses, is infectious.

'The ultimate thing to do would be to ride bareback and bridleless, which I'm almost at. Dallas will stop dead on voice command and when he did that I realised, *Oh yes, I can do this!*

'At the end of the year, the riding school is having a campout near Sorelle where we're just going to ride on the beach and I was like, *Yes! A beach ride is exactly what I've always wanted to do!*

'Actually, at the start of this year I thought, *I'm going to beach ride this year* . . . and now I *am*. On Dallas! It will be amazing.

'So I'm going to work him up to that and go on a few trail rides, just getting in there, and take him to shows, and pony club and jumping – I love jumping! The first time I jumped him he did a marvellous jump and I was like, *Oh, great!* 'Cause I just wanted to get straight into that, so I'll do lots of that this weekend, getting him into jumping . . .'

'Starting low,' reminds Olivia's mother, Vicki Ruzicka.

'Yeah, I can do forty centimetres, only at a trot. He's a bit clumsy still. But he's getting there.

'In my bedroom I've got models of horses, with a black one I called Dallas, and they lie on my bed. I have show ribbons hanging above my bed, dream catchers, horse movies, horse stuffed toys – the *Saddle Club* ones. I've got every single one of them. I have pictures of Stardust and Dallas.

'I live with Mum, Dad, Jon (my oldest brother, he's like, twenty-four), Ben, who's twenty-one, and he's got an apartment in town but he's coming back to live too, and then there's Andrew who is twenty, and then there's Meghan, who's fifteen, who used to be into horses but then got out of it, and I'm still troubled about that to this day. She's more into sports and basketball these days. She'll watch every horse movie with me and she'll love it and we cry over movies but for some reason she just stopped all the horse things and I'm mad at her 'cause I could have my sister to do all this with and that would be amazing. The other day I was looking at horses for sale, I dunno, I just do that sometimes, and she's like, "What about *my* horse?" and I was like, "It's too late for you." And then there's me, the youngest of five kids, and I'll *never* stop loving horses!'

I ask Olivia what it feels like when she's with a horse. She takes several moments, searching for words, until finally settling on the right one.

'Home.'

For eight years, from the age of four to the time Olivia entered high school, she lived and breathed horses and had one clear dream: to go to the high school with the farm. Her mother, Vicki, is a teacher's assistant at the school.

'Until recently, I was also the accredited Riding for Disabled (RDA) coach, Level 1, as well as the accredited pony club coach,' Vicki says. 'The high school ran a farm and on the farm we had cattle and horses and we decided to run an RDA centre because we had a lot of students with disabilities. So we became qualified to do that and we trained our horses to be accredited horses. It's quite stringent. You have to do workshops and study.

'When I first started there, Olivia was in kindergarten and she and her sister were riding the Shetland ponies at shows when they were four and five. I'd take them along every year after that, with a team of horses. She did cattle handling as well. The school had its own Murray Grey stud and we went away on camps and to shows. It was amazing.'

'It was the only school that had a farm, so I was always definitely going there,' Olivia says. 'I've always seen myself being an equine veterinarian or something like that. I can't imagine myself in a job without horses. Even if I got a normal job I'd work part-time and I'd work as hard as I possibly could for anything that has anything to do with horses, even if it's volunteering at the

RSPCA with the rescue horses.'

In the final year of primary school, Olivia had the chance to attend an orientation day at the high school she'd dreamed about for so long.

'Me and my friend Kayleigh had waited and waited ever since we'd met each other. We'd always talked about what we'd do when we got to high school and all the shows we'd go to and what horses we'd ride. And at that first orientation day, we got a taste of what it would be like.

'At recess, we went down to the farm and hopped on my pony, Stardust, without helmets or a bridle and I ran around the paddock and he chased me and then I sat on him and she sat on him and . . . well, I don't think we were really *supposed* to be doing that, but that's what we did and it was *so* much fun!'

Olivia was at the end of Year 6, just about to go to her dream high school, when she heard the farm and horse programs had been cut.

Vicki says, 'The focus changed from a lot of the extra programs we had, such as automotive, the farm, and art. We had a lot of students who weren't really coping academically or in the classroom, and those programs gave them an avenue they could excel in. But they shut the farm down, along with our arena and our round yard. It's horrible now, all grown over.'

'I just lost it when I found out,' Olivia says. 'I cried for days.'

But there was worse to come. When the farm had been a part of the school, Vicki and Olivia were able to have horses of their own and keep them on the farm, and the horses worked in the education program. The Ruzicka family lives on a suburban block right in the middle of Launceston. When the school shut down the farm, they lost the only place they had available to them to keep their horses.

Olivia had had a 24-year-old pony, Stardust, on lease for about a year and a half. 'He was a really good confidence builder. We went to pony club and to a show. He looked after me. He was a great old pony,' she says.

And Vicki had her horse, a nineteen-year-old bay Standardbred called Ben. Vicki had to sell Ben to a student she'd worked with for five years and who had assisted on the farm with the horses.

'She loved him just as much as I did. I couldn't afford to agist him close to me and I just couldn't find anywhere cheaper,' Vicki says.

Meanwhile, Olivia had to return Stardust to his owners. Even now, she gets very emotional when talking about it.

'It's like losing your best friend, like a family member. I haven't seen him since I gave him back. He's probably some other little girl's pony now.'

Olivia entered her first year of high school still heartbroken, her dreams shattered and her horses gone.

'My whole life had been with horses. I really didn't know anything else. That year without horses was really bad.' Her voice breaks. 'I had one friend who had a pony. Kayleigh was the only friend I ever had at school who liked horses. She got a black pony. We would talk about horses all the time but it wasn't really the same because she could talk about her pony but I couldn't. I'd just smile and nod because I didn't really have anything to talk about any more.'

Olivia began to fall into darkness.

'She had a lot of sick days,' Vicki said. 'I cried a lot. I was worried sick. So was her teacher.'

Alison Johnson was Olivia's teacher that year and shared Vicki's concern for Olivia.

'Olivia started the year off well; however, during term two she began to withdraw from her friends and her studies. She had many days off, or would often go home sick part way through the day. I saw this beautiful, friendly, happy young lady starting to slip further and further into herself. She was quieter than normal in class and she started to look quite pale. I had numerous conversations with Vicki throughout this time about Olivia and how she was feeling, most often ending up with Vicki, and sometimes myself, in tears.

'Vicki and I discussed the idea of counselling and the family also got a puppy, which seemed to brighten Olivia up when she spoke of it and when she brought it into the classroom some mornings.

'Olivia's attendance was significantly affected by her mental wellbeing in Grade 7. She's a very bright and capable young lady, which meant that she didn't fall behind, but if she wasn't so bright this would have definitely been the case.

'She was deeply saddened that the farm was no longer an option for her and she was finding it hard to get motivated after the animals had all been removed. She was also in a small friendship group of three girls, which at times saw her being left out a little, or feeling as if she was being left out. It took a long time for us to pinpoint what was going on, though, and Olivia struggled for a while to get across to us what exactly was happening with her.'

'I'd always had headaches but they were occurring more,' Olivia says.

Vicki says, 'That year was difficult for her. The headaches were coming on more severely. She didn't want to go to school. We had a lot of trouble getting her there. And then when she was there, she was always coming up to me (because I work at the school too), saying, "Can I go home?" and "Please let me go home." Her confidence was gone.'

Fortunately for everyone concerned, the Ruzickas' luck changed. The student who had bought Vicki's horse, Ben, kept him for twelve months until she lost her job and couldn't afford to keep him any more. She phoned Vicki to see if Ben could go back to her. As far as good timing goes, this was the best. A teacher who worked at the school now had some land within walking distance from the Ruzickas' home and offered it as free agistment for Vicki's horse. Olivia's life changed in an instant.

Vicki says, 'Olivia was very excited to be able to come up to the paddock and jump up on Big Ben, but he's 16.1 hands high so he's a bit much for her. He used to work at the school in the RDA program. He lived to work. He used to be at the gate every morning, waiting for the students to bring him down. He used to put his head right down for the kids in wheelchairs so they could touch his ears.'

Now that Ben was back in the family, and the acreage was sorted out for them, Olivia wasted no time in looking for another horse.

'I was on every website I could find, looking for a horse,' she says.

'She was driving us crazy on the net. She would find this

horse, she would find that horse, and we had to ring, and she was just driving us crazy.'

In the end it was the family's farrier who found Dallas for them.

'When our farrier started describing Dallas we just got so excited, but his case was going through the courts so the RSPCA couldn't give us any details. All we knew was that he was thirteen and he did race as a pacer,' Vicki says.

Carrie Palmer from Tasmania's RSPCA says that Dallas was originally seized, and later surrendered by his previous owner. He was seized due to issues of neglect, with a light bodyweight, internal and external parasites and significant hair loss.

Dallas was rescued in September 2012 and came to the Ruzickas' in February 2013.

Carrie says that the Ruzickas were a 'beautiful, caring and compassionate family who were keen to continue his rehabilitation and were the perfect match for Dallas.'

'He was described to us as having the most incredible temperament,' Vicki says. 'He just put up with everything they did to him to improve his health with such gentleness. And he is still like that now. He's just so grateful.

'There was a moment early on, when he hadn't been with us for long. We put his food down and turned to leave. But instead of gulping it down like he usually did, like a starved horse would, he actually left his feed and walked up to Olivia and put his head over her shoulder and just rested there. It was such a touching moment. We're sure he was saying thank you.

'We've taken his training slowly because when you get a rescue horse, you've no idea what they know and what they don't know. So you just have to start at the beginning.'

Olivia says she was speechless when she first saw Dallas. She couldn't believe he could really be hers.

'I instantly thought of all the things we could do together, riding and going places. I loved him straight away. He was in a paddock with a little filly that had also been rescued. He came straight up to us. The filly would sniff us and then run away. But he stayed and let us brush him and put the halter on, put a saddle on him. He followed me around in the paddock like a puppy. He rolled in the paddock and then just sat there on his haunches like a dog!'

Dallas didn't know how to trot any more. As a racing pacer, his natural trotting gait had been forced out of him. Pacers race in a harness like trotters but, unlike trotters, the gait is unnatural. A pacer has to move its left front and hind foot at the same time, then the right front and hind foot together, rather than the natural trotting gait of opposite front and hind feet together. This gait is held together by hopples strapped around their legs. Dallas had to learn to trot all over again.

'It's the fear thing,' Vicki says. 'Some trainers can be really hard on the pacers and they're too scared to do anything else. But now he's more relaxed. And we don't use a bit; we use a bitless bridle so he relaxes his head down. He's just working beautifully now.'

Vicki and Olivia say they 'do a bit of everything' when it comes to horse training.

'Mostly natural,' Vicki says. 'We ride English style. We don't ride western. But still love western riding. We love all riding. You can take a little bit from everything but the biggest thing is that everything is natural. Even when we move our horses around, it's all done naturally. There's no force. Everything is pressure and release. No metal bits. You find that when you ride them in a bitless bridle for a while they relax into a natural carriage. They find that they're using themselves a lot better and they don't have to fidget and worry about a bit. So that stress goes.'

Olivia says, 'I was worried about that with Dallas 'cause I didn't know if he'd ever really been yanked on the bit.'

'We didn't even try him in a bit. It was straight into the bitless bridle and he just took to it like a duck to water,' Vicki says.

'I can ride him bareback in the paddock in a halter now. I'm not really aged or experienced enough to take on a green horse to retrain or anything, but it hasn't been as hard as I thought it would be, actually.' Olivia smiles with pride.

Her teacher Alison says she's seen the change in Olivia since Dallas has been in her life.

'Today, Olivia is a different student to the one she was last year. I walk into her class, she is laughing, having fun, being a teenager. She is blossoming with her studies and she is healthy and active. She is even participating in more sports teams with her friends this year and really getting in and enjoying it.'

Olivia agrees life is much better. 'I'm definitely happier. Before Dallas, after school I wouldn't really have much to do, now I'm just begging to go down to Dallas all the time. I'll walk if I have to but it's hard to carry a saddle in your bag.'

And it seems even her school life has improved.

'School's not as bad as I thought it was going to be. On Tuesdays I walk straight to Dallas even if it's really cold and I'm only wearing one of those winter skirts and ballet flats. Sometimes my friends will come and I will just jump on him and sit on him while he grazes.

'Now we talk about what rugs we've bought. We get on the iPads at school and show each other which rugs we got and what colour and where we got them from.'

Olivia's favourite subjects are music, art and photography.

'I've got all these ideas of photos I'm going to take with Dallas. I have a really great camera. My brother bought it for me for my birthday. That was when I had no horses so there was no horsey thing to buy.'

Olivia began going to a riding school before she got Dallas and now goes there with him too.

'The first time I went to the riding school everyone was so nice. I got my choice of horses to ride. I fell in love with this Standardbred called Jack. But he got an injury in the paddock and he's still injured and I can't ride him any more. I'm taking Dallas up there on the holidays and I'll just ride him around up there, which will be great because they've got some great riding areas. I mean, no indoor arenas or anything that big, but paddocks. They've got a good hundred acres to trail ride in and great jumping paddocks. Last Saturday, they had a fun day with an obstacle course and activities and that sort of thing so I felt like I was back at pony club. I wasn't able to do it on Dallas – he wasn't quite up to that yet 'cause of things like balloons popping, and I didn't want him to go through a bad experience quite yet. I want to build him up to something like that. We're doing pretty well.'

'We just don't want to rush him,' Vicki says. 'So he'll go down there and spend a day just walking around and have a gentle time and then she'll get on him and do a few little things and then just see how much he can cope with. I think he'll do well. We've already taken him down there for a day trip and he did so well.'

'It's pretty crazy down there. It's near the airport so there are planes flying over your head every few minutes and trains going past,' Olivia says.

'Our dream, and we're working on it right now, we're at the very beginning, is using the horses – Dallas, Ben and maybe a couple of rescue ponies from the RSPCA – and have a small team to use as therapy,' Vicki says. 'We're looking at kids in the foster system. But it won't be a part of the high school; it will be a separate thing. So we're hoping to branch out and use the animals as therapy.'

The seven members of the Ruzicka family, along with all the animals, live in a three-bedroom house, with the garage converted into another bedroom.

'I've got a golden retriever that I used to take to the school and he worked with autistic boys,' Vicki says. 'He was fantastic around kids. All the animals we had on the farm, except the cattle, are here with me: the rabbits, the guinea pigs, as well as two fat cats that we rescued from the Hobart RSPCA and two dogs – Beau and Hilfie. Hilfie is a border collie with ADHD. He's a special needs dog. He's very affectionate with people but can't handle other dogs and is not good with cars.'

On the day I visit them, the house is open and warm, with people moving from room to room and an adopted stray black kitten playing on the couch. A lost dog is also waiting inside the house until its owner can be found. Vicki seems in her element in this environment.

'Our next goal is a stable,' Vicki says.

'Oh, yeah,' Olivia chimes in. 'My friend Gemma went to AgFest with her family and they got an awesome stable thing they've got in their yard. After riding school one day I went home with them to their place and she has a miniature pony, Honey, who we don't ride, and then there's Patchy, who is a stereotypical Shetland pony, seriously. We put him in the stable and were feeding him and we didn't have him tied up or anything and we put the light on so we could see most of the things we were doing, and we were just doing little things like standing up on him, and we were timing how fast we could do that round-the-world thing [a game where you sit on a horse, spin yourself around to face the rump and then spin again to face the front]. Gemma started at ten seconds, then we worked on it for an hour, and we got her down to 3.4 seconds, and I got to 2.9 and I was so excited. And the whole time, he would just sit there and eat.'

'Aren't they tolerant, these little ponies?' Vicki says in admiration.

Olivia reflects on the difficult year before she had Dallas.

'There was nothing really at school that was a problem. I guess I just didn't want to go to school and not go to the farm. I hadn't pictured my life any other way and it was hard to think about what was going to happen. I went. But my attendance was pretty bad that year. Most days I had to go home with a headache or take Panadol.

'I'm still friends with Kayleigh and Brianna. And me and Kayleigh talk about horses, and sometimes we get Brianna talking about horses and that's good. And I have this friend, Alana, I talk about horses with her, she's probably sick of it, but I always talk about horses, and she's really smart and has me focusing on school again. She's got one of those families where all her sisters have grown up and are doing amazing things. One of her sisters is in the navy and travelling the world, and that's what she wants to do too, help the world, or forensic science.

'That first year at high school was hard, but I always had really good friends who let me ride their horses. And later on in that year, I was able to go to Gemma's and play with their ponies. They're out in Evandale with a river and kayaks and paddocks. It's like the dream. Their house has grapevines growing around it. Seriously! They have no idea how great it is. They have sheep and lambs that come up and will jump in your arms. So that helped. It helped having really good friends that would distract me and keep me going.'

And the dream of another horse helped too.

'I always knew one day I'd get a horse. I knew I wouldn't go the rest of my life without having another horse; I just didn't know when it would be. It was overwhelming when I found out we could have Ben back and immediately I began searching for another horse. Mum wouldn't let me ride Ben all the time. *She* wanted to ride him! And anyway, he's too full of himself. He knows I'm too little to do anything major with him.'

It's clear that life is moving forward for both Olivia and Vicki, in all sorts of exciting ways.

'We have all these new relationships with lovely people who have big hearts for horses,' Vicki says. 'Horses that would have ended up in a can are now having new lives. And we're just a small part of that. And having Dallas has enriched us . . . I can't even describe it. Every time I see him, I just think we're so lucky that we've been able to adopt a horse and give him such a home.'

Carrie from the RSPCA says, 'It's amazing that Dallas has progressed into such a wonderfully loyal and trusting horse. Olivia and Vicki have brought out the best in him. They deserve to live long happy lives in each other's company. I *love* getting updates and photos from his new family. It makes it all worthwhile to see an animal finally find health and happiness.'

Dallas's case has now been through the courts.

The RSPCA says that in March 2014 a woman was convicted in the Launceston Magistrates Court for the offences of inappropriately managing three horses. The penalty issued was a $750 fine, a custody capping order, which means the magistrate has permitted her to have no more than seven horses for a period of three years, and to reimburse the RSPCA for costs incurred.

HORSES FOR HOPE

Michael Williams has spent more than a third of his life passing in and out of prison but is now a man who, finally, knows a little bit about hope.

'I just got married to Kathy. That's probably the highlight of my life, apart from when my son was born. He's seventeen now and I had him when I was a kid. But the highlight of my adult life was getting back with my fiancée and then marrying her. We met in 2001 and my life was still going in the wrong direction. I didn't want to take her down that path with me and we split ways. I knew back then that she was the right type of girl to spend my life with but I didn't want to damage her or hurt her so I went my own way. It was only through chance that I managed to catch up with her again. I had tried several times over the years but was unsuccessful. She's been my saving grace. She's my rock. She never judges me. She saved me from the life I was living, and if there is such a thing as "the one" then I think I've found her.'

But life hasn't always been so joyful.

'I grew up in a very violent home. I had an alcoholic father. My mum used to cop a beating ten out of seven days. Being the only boy, I tried to look after my older sister (the middle child), and my other sister (the eldest) tried to look after us younger ones. But we saw a lot of things that kids should never see. I started losing friends of mine to suicide when I was twelve and thirteen years old. I turned to drugs and fighting. If I didn't get in half a dozen fights in a weekend then that was a bad weekend. I got to the point that I enjoyed hurting other people.

'But my biggest downfall was heroin.'

Drug-related offences lead to Michael's twelve years through the prison system.

'I got involved very deeply with heroin by the time I was sixteen, and I had my son not long after. I pulled up for a bit at that time but I went back to the drugs and my son ended up with my mother, where he still is, though he stays with me a fair bit now. He's a brilliant kid. He just finished Year 12. He's extremely smart and will be taking a gap year and then going to uni. My mum's done a fantastic job with him.'

But the pain of not being there for his son is still raw.

'It was really hard, dealing with the fact that I watched my son grow up via the visitor centre in prison. Every time I saw him, he'd grown and developed further since the last month. It was hell.

'When I got out of jail the first time, every single thing I'd known before I went in was gone. All my so-called friends were gone. My family home had been sold so I never actually got to go home. On the day I left jail, I found out my dad had cancer and was going in for an operation. I got out of jail and was bombarded with so many things. In comparison, learning to live in jail was so much easier than learning to live in the real world again.

'I still struggle so much with where do I fit, where do I go, where do I belong, how do I do this? A couple of months ago, I paid my first-ever bill in thirty-four years. I could have just let it go (it was already a default on my credit rating) but I *wanted* to pay it. So I did. And it was my first ever bill and it felt good to be able to do that.'

During Michael's time in prison, he says he was fortunate to have been able to work with horses through the Uniting Care 'Cutting Edge' program, Horses for Hope, in Shepparton, Victoria. Cutting Edge's programs include youth services, refugee assistance, alternative education programs and Horses for Hope. Horses for Hope is possibly most well known for the work it did with survivors of the Victorian bushfires, though clients from all walks of life benefit from its service.

Colin Emonson and Tiffany Peverall are the co-founders of Horses for Hope. Tiffany now lives overseas and Colin remains the manager and primary provider of the therapeutic service, along with practitioner Alison Pozzobon and two volunteers who work two days a week each at the centre.

Colin says, 'My career has been driven by believing there has to be better ways of engaging young people, the abused and traumatised. As a society, we don't do a very good job with them. It's not about them; it's about us. And we should be doing a better job for them as a community.

'Horses for Hope gives me more than I give it. I say that we've got the best job in the world. Every day we see horses healing. Every day we see people healing. Every day we experience those very real connections that happen between a horse and a person and we facilitate those. And it doesn't get any better than that. The energy that I bring to this job and my commitment is all about that.'

The prisoners who attend the program are all pre-release prisoners.

'They're the ones who are getting ready to be discharged. So they're getting ready to have this huge change, from living in the style you have to live in the prison and all the things you have to do to survive there, to making a huge flip and being able to fit in with your family and community. And they are diametrically opposed, those two things. Horses for Hope helps them understand and manage what's going on emotionally, which is a very different way of doing things than in prison.'

Horses for Hope is unique in that the horses come for healing at the same time as the people, but they are essentially on loan to Colin and his team. At its best it's a win-win for all parties, but it doesn't come without difficulty.

'The horses are owned by various people and they come into the program for healing as well. But their levels of fear or sensitivity decline through their own therapy and they're therefore not as valuable to us therapeutically once they've lost their fear, so they need to be able to go home.

'It costs a lot to have the horses in the program. It would be cheaper for us to have our own horses to use, but then we wouldn't get the therapeutic value from them because they wouldn't be so sensitive. Uniting Care has been very generous and directed a lot of funds our way, but wherever possible, people pay to have their horses in the program. Still, there are a lot of horses out there that would really benefit from the therapy but their owners can't afford to pay. And a lot of our horses were rescued by the current owners in the first place. We're cautious to ensure the horses have a place to go home to after the program and we work with the owners to make sure they've got the skills and knowledge to continue to help the horses once they are home.'

Just as many of the clients who come to Horses for Hope are at risk, so too are the horses.

'Most of those horses, without some kind of intervention or some kind of change, were either going to live out their lives in their paddock untouched and neglected, or were going to end up at the dogger's. We try to keep it to ten horses in the program at a time, but usually end up with fifteen.'

Horses stay from a few weeks to twelve months, depending on their issue.

'We work with the horse from the absolute beginning through to accepting a saddle, or walking on tarps, or whatever the owner thought was the problem in the first place. If a client's been in the program for a while, they will have gone through a whole range of experiences with the horse. Connecting with the horse is the starting point but they'll move on to different and more challenging tasks. We assess a horse when it first comes in to see where it's up to and figure out what its needs are, to ensure it's going to be safe. We work with a horse to the point where we think it's going to be listening and safe and then we'll leave all the rest of the training to people in the program.'

Michael says, 'The first time we went out there, we drove up and I remember thinking, *What are we doing here? What are we in for? What have we signed up for?* Then we found out that these were all ex-racehorses or horses that had been abused or got injuries, and then we put on these big vests and helmets and it felt like, *Christ, we're going to get killed in here!*'

Horses for Hope is the culmination of many years of research and practice for Colin.

'I've been in the youth and family field for thirty years, mostly working with high-risk kids. I've always had a strong interest in therapeutic approaches, especially in narrative therapy. I was a farmer, and always bred and trained horses. I developed an interest in the Monty Roberts method of horsemanship, developed skills and came up with the idea of combining narrative therapy and equine communication.

'We take each client through the process of replicating herd leadership. When a horse comes across something new or something it finds scary, we say that is hard and tricky for them. What we want the person in the yard to do is take on a form of leadership that we call 'shepherd leadership' – communicating without force to help horses, shepherd them, through those hard and tricky situations.

'The person involved first has to understand that process, has to understand the communication that's going on, and then spends fifteen minutes with the horse, communicating with it as a leader. They take the horse from seeing the person as a predator, as they naturally do, through to adopting that person into the herd. It's palpable. You not only see it; you can feel it. Even people who don't know horses can feel or notice the difference between the horse that is running away in fear and the horse that approaches in a very calm state and seeks leadership. We're aiming to get people to see that within themselves they have things that are normally not seen or not recognised, and that they could use these things and bring them forward to influence a problem.

'For example, someone who has anger management problems invariably has trouble identifying when strong feelings come along, and they don't believe that they can change or manage those feelings. Anybody who steps into the yard with a horse is going to experience strong feelings, such as nervousness or anxiety. When they're successful in getting a horse to come to them instead of running away, they have an experience of controlling things they normally feel they can't control. So in the therapeutic process we aim to develop that and see where it fits into their life.'

Colin makes it clear there is no 'magic' that happens when you put a person with a horse. In other words, there is real work involved here. 'The horsemanship skills and the follow-up narrative therapy are what create the outcomes.'

Colin explains that narrative therapy 'starts from the assumption that it's not the person that's the problem; it's the problem that's the problem. This person is affected by this problem more so than the person actually *being* the problem. They don't actually want this problem. They'd prefer not to have it around.

'Change occurs when the client can identify that the personal story they're carrying inside themselves might not be quite right.

'The simplest and best example I can give you is the kids who come along with a learning difficulty. They think, *Well, I'm probably not going to do well with this*. We put them in a situation where they need to learn some fairly intricate stuff about horses. We help them, they don't have to do it all from memory, but we teach them a lot, like that horses see people as predators; and herd leadership issues, how a herd leader manages the herd, the communication that occurs between horses, and so forth.

'So they get in the yard and they learn how to communicate as a leader and make a physical and emotional connection with the horse. And they'll come back next week, and we'll say, "Now, we know learning's a bit difficult . . .", and we'll go over the information again. And invariably they'll start to say, "Yeah, I know, I remember that, yeah, yeah," and we'll say, "What do you mean? What's going on here? You told me you had difficulties in learning. What's happened here? Did you learn all this?" And suddenly they'll start to think, *Hang on, maybe I'm a learner, not a non-learner, but maybe there are some things getting in the road*. That's something within themselves. We're not telling them, we're just creating space for them to learn those things.

'That's a very simple story. Every horse-yard experience brings with it those realisations, and the narrative therapy process enables us to draw those out. We start with people for whom the problem has great influence on their life and they have very little influence on the life of the problem, and by the time we're finished we want that to be flipped over.'

With the horse playing such a crucial role in the therapeutic process, Colin and Alison have to carefully consider which horse is matched with which client.

'That's so critical to what we do.'

So far, they've never had to reject a horse for the program.

'People ask what we do when we have a bad horse. But my view of horses is exactly the same as my view of people: there are no bad horses, there are only horses with bad experiences. The riskiest horse we took on was an ex-racehorse. She'd never made it to the racetrack but she'd been trained for that, and was physically and quite emotionally damaged by that process. They couldn't get her to us; they couldn't get her on the truck because they were scared she was going to kill someone – literally.

'We don't claim to be experts or gurus but we like to try to work through problems. So we went down and spent time with her, using the shepherd leadership techniques just as we teach clients to do, and loaded her differently (from the front, not from behind) and she walked on the float. I'm not saying that would work every time but it did in this case and she went on to work with kids. But you wouldn't want to get someone stuck behind her, putting pressure on her, because that was her problem. Everything in the past had been done from behind – into the barriers, into the float, whacked from behind – she just went into defensive mode. It's just a matter of understanding that horse. I don't know if there are horses out there that couldn't be in the program. I haven't met any yet.

'We had a two year old come to us after being through two trainers. This horse would get really frustrated when you tried to teach him something and when he got frustrated he would get angry, and when he got angry he would get a bit dangerous and he would rear and strike and so on. We actually discovered that we had to teach him more slowly. And once we broke it down, he was absolutely fine. He works with our little kids now. We're hanging on to him because he was one of those *well, what will we do with him?* cases, but he actually has a good role to play, being able to work with really small children.'

Michael's first experience was with a horse called Belle.

'I loved Belle. I think I felt a connection in some way with her.

She'd taken off from her handler and gotten caught up in barbed wire and tore herself to bits. It was like I could see her pain in her eyes and, I don't know – this is going to sound like I'm a nutcase – but it was as though she knew I had pain too. It was like we related. It was like a mutual respect. All the horses were great, but she was the first horse I worked with, so I think that played a big part.'

For Michael, the Horses for Hope program was an unexpected experience that he says has had deep, long-lasting effects in his life.

'When I was at Dhurringile, a minimum-security jail, I saw the poster advertising that there were positions open for this program. I'm an animal person but I'd never really had anything to do with horses. But something just drew me to it. We had a meeting with some of the prison staff and Colin and then we had to write a bit of an essay about why we wanted to be a part of it and why we should be given the opportunity. I wanted to learn something from it and take something out of it. At that point in my life I was well and truly over jail. I didn't want jail to be my life. I didn't want to keep going in and out as I'd done for the past twelve years or so and I wanted to try anything. I just felt there was something there.

'We went through an interview process and they asked lots of questions. You had to be at a level where you could leave the prison without a security guard going with you and I think they were worried about people wanting to do it just to get out for the day and muck around and not take it seriously. They were pretty full-on with the selection process. I was rapt when I got the green light to be a part of it.

'We went every second Friday over three or four months. The prison itself made it very difficult for us to go because they thought of it as a day out where we were getting privilege. The process we had to go through to be involved was quite lengthy. It was a daunting experience. I'm not used to that sort of thing, especially inside a jail. But it was well and truly worth every minute of it.'

Colin, too, has experienced difficulties working in the prison system.

'I think some of the prison staff have reservations about the program and maybe see it as a reward for the prisoners, so they're not entirely okay about it. Obviously, not everybody's like that, but it's a complex system to work within.'

Michael is quite clear about how the program helped him.

'It was a massive confidence-builder, in the sense that you can get someone to trust you and you're worthy of someone trusting you. After all the years I spent in jail, I started to doubt that I was worthy of anything. I didn't believe that I was worthy of anyone's love or trust or respect, but within ten or fifteen minutes in the yard, this beast that's been abused or hurt or scared of people or whatever else, within fifteen-odd minutes, that animal trusts you. It was a profound experience. I was on a high for two weeks afterwards and couldn't wait to get back. I so looked forward to being there every second Friday; it was the highlight of every fortnight. The team out there was fantastic. They didn't judge us at all. They helped us through it.

'There was one activity we did where we had to, as a group, get the horses to go through obstacles and jump, and do it all without talking. And once again, to learn that you can work as a team – that we're not just numbers and we can get past what we've become – it was amazing. In the jail system, they work very hard at stripping you down and making you feel like you're nothing and that you can't lead anything and you can't be responsible for anything. But within two or three sessions of being involved with these horses, I started to realise that I can change and that I can be in control of my destiny. I *can* change this.

'It changed my outlook on so many things. I honestly believe it did play a big part in me being able to turn my life around.

'I finished the course in December 2010 and then got out in January 2011. I brought so much home with me. Just that confidence . . . it was really the confidence. I do still struggle a great deal with being out of my comfort zone socially. We went to a wedding earlier in the year and I knew the bride and groom well enough but I knew no one else there. I felt so uncomfortable and on edge all night, but I could handle it because I'd stepped into that horse arena, totally out of my comfort zone, and I'd been able to handle that. It just taught me that I can overcome my fears and I can work with myself through anything. I've been able to apply that, consciously or subconsciously, since I've been out. And I haven't looked back. I've had a few stumbles but I've managed to get straight back on my feet. A lot of that has to do with my wife. But I could sit here all day and go on and on about the things I took away from that program.'

For Colin, the seeds of Horses for Hope took root many years ago.

'In terms of my own experiences with horses, I went through a period of about three years of quite serious illness, and three major operations. Horses were important for me in that when I had a little bit of energy I would go and spend time with a horse. I hadn't considered them as part of the healing process, necessarily, but they were always there and I would enjoy them and feel good about it. I have a stallion that's twelve now and a pretty nice horse and I'd just go out and spend time with him. Horses for Hope grew out of that period.

'It was a chance to reflect and think about life and what's important. Tiff and I had actually played with the idea of Horses for Hope before then, but during that period I had more time to think about it, experiment with it and research it. And also to make some decisions about what was important to me. I think of that period of time as quite a gift.

'The horses are a fundamental part of what we do. And unless we do it right for the horses, and take care of their needs, nothing else will work, so this is about their needs and their healing, certainly. But we wouldn't be running Horses for Hope just for the horses. We are here to help heal as many people as possible.

'Being with a horse can provide peace and stimulation and a whole range of things that are helpful and can be healing. But it's the context we put around it, it's what the person understands, and it's creating the environment where they connect and feel unique things and feel them really powerfully that, *together* with the horse, creates the results.

'I would do this work for nothing and I have done. A while back, we nearly lost the whole program because we just didn't have enough income, so I worked for three days a week for six months without pay. And I don't have any regrets about that because this program is too valuable to lose for the sake of me not getting paid.

'There are people in my life who describe the Horses for Hope program as "spirit-driven". I'm not sure how I feel about that term but it certainly feels as though there is something driving me here. This is the most effective thing I've done by a long shot. My goal in life at this stage is to see this program being made available to other people, purely because it is valuable and worthwhile for people who can't get help in other ways.'

Colin's passion and commitment to the Horses for Hope program is unquestionable. A humble man by nature (who is deeply uncomfortable with the attention on himself), he is driven not by financial gain or personal recognition, but by the desire to see as many people as possible have access to the program, regardless of whether or not they can afford it. It's not about him and what he can get from it; it's about what he can give and leave behind.

'I have some views about the individual not being as important as the community, and I think that we as a community need to be looking after each other more so than looking after ourselves. I do come from a religious family background and those beliefs are very strongly tied in with that sense of community and doing the right thing.'

And he's not slowing down any time soon.

'I'm having way too much fun to retire. I will slow down at some stage and I'd like to go and do some things like see a bit more of Australia, but I have no intentions of retiring yet. I have a little farm and I run horses on my farm, so there're always things to do. I will continue to work on this.'

Horses for Hope does, as the name suggests, offer hope, both to horses and the people who work with them. But there are no quick fixes, as both Colin and Michael well know.

'This program doesn't fix everything,' Colin says. 'It doesn't cure mental illness. But what it does is give people a chance to look at things differently.'

For Michael, heroin continues to be his biggest challenge.

'For a long time, I was alone and the only refuge I had was heroin. It was the only constant that was in my life from before I went to jail to when I came home. Nothing else was the same.

'I'm trying to turn my life around as best as I can. It's taking a bit of time but I keep going and hopefully I'll get there.

'I'm on the methadone program. I go and pick that up every day and I know I'm a long way from stopping. I don't know when I'm going to be able to stop. The goal is to have it done by June or July next year, but who knows? It might take longer, it might be sooner. I got down to a low dose but started using again so I went back to my doctor and asked to increase it. I said I was struggling, I was using, I didn't know why but I needed to go back up. I wanted to nip it in the bud before it became jail or a full-blown habit once more.

'It's very scary and it's hard. It's very scary for Kat. She's as straight as they come and doesn't understand where I'm at. The difference between ten years ago, when I would have been out robbing everything, to the fact that now I go to work five or six days a week driving semi-trailers to make money . . . it's big.

'If there was an operation you could have that would cut that part of your brain out, but there was only a 30 per cent chance you'd live, I would take that chance. I just want it gone. I am so, so sick of it. I've had enough. I want my family. I want a job. I want the heroin gone. It scares me so badly that I can't make it go.

'But the program has helped me believe in myself enough that I think I *can* get a job, I *am* worthy, I'm *not* the scum of the earth, and I *can* be in society. I hold that inside me and take it wherever I go and it's up to me to use it. It's like that old saying: you can lead a horse to water but you can't make him drink. At the end of the day, everything's about what you want to do and how much you're willing to do it.'

Colin says, 'Whether I'm riding a horse or working with it on the ground, the sense that comes from those moments when you are truly connected is just mind-blowing. It's hard to describe. There's a great pleasure in it, but there's more than that. Oneness is a great word. Bliss is a great word too. You don't have to be riding a horse to get that. You can walk in a paddock and get that. My work is all about trying to enable people to have that experience and then using the therapeutic process to the max for the greatest possible change.'

There's no doubt that with continued support from Uniting Care Cutting Edge and Colin at the helm of Horses for Hope, more people like Michael will have breakthroughs to new possibilities and the chance to write themselves a new story, bringing much-needed hope to their lives.

JOLEENA

When Alwyn and I first met Joleena, she was standing in a slaughterhouse holding yard, up to her fetlocks in black stinking mud, staring vacantly ahead, chewing unenthusiastically on mouldy straw, flies crawling over her slim frame, with her young colt beside her.

I climbed into the pen with my heart pounding as it always did when I walked through clusters of horses on death row. Some horses had black tags around their necks, a signal they weren't to be sold to anyone but were for slaughter only. One of these horses was a tall, emaciated, flea-bitten grey gelding with a broken pelvis, waiting for his suffering to end.

Taking steadying breaths above the pain in my chest, I focused on Joleena and her colt. On this day, it was them I was there to save, not the dozens of other horses stoically awaiting their fate. We were also taking another mare and foal. All we knew about them was that they had both come from the same stud and the foals were the same age. It was January and hot. Sweat trickled down my back and I picked my way carefully through the slop in the yard.

I stood next to Joleena and waited for the horse transport. Intense unease swept over me, a wary instinct preventing me from reaching out to touch her. She made no acknowledgement of my presence – no flick of an ear, no turn of the head, no flutter of an eye. She was dark bay, her summer coat nearly black, and she emanated a mood just as black, a barbed warning to anyone who ventured near to keep well away. The rectangular white brand running parallel to her mane indicated that she was a Standardbred – the breed used for trotting races.

Her young foal was limping with an unknown injury in a foreleg, the cause of which was impossible to decipher given the depth of mud he was standing in. It could have been anything – a birth deformity, an abscess, a torn tendon. For the purpose of this rescue, it didn't change our immediate actions. When we set out to rescue a horse we took them on and committed to them, regardless of the issues they came with. And as was the case with almost all rescues, either no one knew the horse's history or they did know but were unlikely to tell the truth. It was better off just to start again.

Joleena was underweight, but not nearly as badly as I'd seen in the past and certainly not as badly as many of the horses around her. Her hooves, from what I could see as she stamped in irritation at the flies, were overgrown and obviously untended for a long time, which seemed to be par for the course with all rescues. There was mud plastered all over her body and matting her long mane, but that was all superficial. I assumed she would have terrible teeth, her dental work likely unattended to for some time as well. And she likely had worms. Nothing out of the ordinary so far.

Her colt was a good-looking young thing. He still had his baby coat, but it had started to moult, and going by that I estimated his age to be around two months. He was also a bit thin and the moulting chestnut coat didn't help his shabby look. But his eyes were bright and he didn't look sickly, just lame on that foreleg, something we could hopefully help.

As I watched, he moved up to Joleena's side for a drink, raising his soft grey lips to her teats. Quick as lightning, she booted him with her back leg, hitting his small frame with a sickening thump, sending him spinning across the yard.

My instincts telling me to keep my distance had been right. Joleena may have been a survivor, but she was also a fighter.

Joleena understood humans only through the eyes of an animal of prey. To her, humans were predators who could hunt, hurt and kill her.

When threatened or stressed in any way, horses have three options for self-preservation: freeze, flight, or fight. Most horses will choose flight as the first port of call, hence why horses are fast gallopers. A healthy horse can mostly always outrun its predator. If a horse feels trapped or cornered, it may choose to fight, with its weapons of choice being its feet and teeth and the ability to rear and buck to dislodge an animal clinging to its back (including a rider). If it is stuck, say, in mud or down a well, or is too unwell to fight or flee, the last option the horse has is to freeze.

A horse is equipped with big, fast reactions, and Joleena was a stressed and frightened horse. She was utterly terrified of being touched in any way. Even eye contact was too much for her and she would turn either her face or whole body away, preferably with her rump (the kicking end) towards you. In response to prolonged stress in her life, she had learned to fight.

My husband, Alwyn, is a physiotherapist with a special interest in cases that are often labelled 'challenging' or 'difficult'. His great passion is for seeking the keys to unlock a client's pain or delayed healing. And it was his experiences with Joleena – an equine fighter and animal of prey – that opened the window on a whole new depth of appreciation for the therapist–client relationship.

'A sick or injured person who ends up in the medical system can have a lot in common with a frightened horse,' Alwyn says. 'On a primal level, the person is already weaker and therefore has less power. Add to that unfamiliar environments, medical terminology they don't understand, a rushed doctor, the fear they might never get better or return to work, and loss of income, and you can have a pretty highly stressed individual. And when you're stressed, it affects your decision-making.'

Similarly, a horse that feels threatened will likely open their eyes very wide (to see as much as they can of their surroundings), raise their head straight up in the air (which gives them superior mono-focal vision to take in long distances and potential threats), and essentially stop 'thinking' and start 'reacting' with their primal brain. One of the foundation blocks of natural horsemanship is to help the horse relax and lower its head because it is only in this position that they can actually think, process and reason. In other words, a horse with its head in the air is not thinking and is certainly not listening you.

Faced with a horse like Joleena, Alwyn says he could see quite quickly and clearly how horses that have been through trauma react a lot like humans who've been through trauma.

In the three years that I ran a rescue organisation I came to see Joleena's story as typical of many broodmares. A breeding stud operates to make money and for many of those businesses (certainly not all), a broodmare becomes just one part of the equation in those operating costs. It's an expensive activity to breed a horse well, taking care of all parties involved and maintaining high levels of quality at every stage. From the many broodmares I encountered, it seems that it becomes tempting for some studs to cut corners along the way.

Almost every week I received desperate pleas from someone trying to save the life of a broodmare on her way to slaughter because her 'usefulness' had expired. Horses are expensive to maintain and most people only want a horse they can ride. A twelve- or twenty-year-old broodmare (usually a Thoroughbred or Standardbred) with no real education, possibly with injuries (often sustained through breeding and foaling – a cracked pelvis, torn ligaments or internal damage isn't unusual), bad feet, a high need for food (as seems to go hand in hand with Thoroughbreds), and often a (totally understandable) 'bad attitude' after their experiences, makes them near impossible to rehome.

Joleena was no different in this regard. When the vet looked at her teeth for a routine dental examination and grinding, she said they appeared not to have been treated in many years, if at all. Her feet, too, had clearly not been treated in a considerable time. Joleena happened to be blessed with wonderfully strong hooves, but they still needed trimming to ensure their health and a correct walking pattern, and to help prevent problems (such as abscesses, seedy toe or laminitis) that we then might not be able to treat. And it was when we tried to have a farrier look at her feet that we began to see the extent of Joleena's trauma.

Her terror of being touched and handled meant we could really only comfortably put a halter on her, and that was only after we'd caught her using food as a bribe. As soon as we started to pat her neck or mane or shoulder, her body became rigid, her nostrils began to flare and she would shift away from us, shrinking under our touch or moving away. If you kept going, you'd be greeted by snapping teeth or striking hooves. Joleena was especially defensive with anyone approaching or touching her anywhere around her rump or back end. Her motto was very much 'attack first and ask questions later'. This of course extended to her legs.

Logically, if you cannot touch a horse's leg comfortably then your chances of picking up the hoof and spending ten or fifteen minutes with it in your hand or between your knees while you nip away hoof wall and rasp it with a metal file are close to none. We began to think Joleena had never had her feet done in her life. As well, we'd rescued a second mare (Shona) and foal at the same time as Joleena (all from the same stud) and the mares' physical condition and fears were nearly identical.

An online studbook register revealed some of the mares' history. We learned they were twelve years old. Joleena had seven recorded foal births in the studbook register. But that wouldn't necessarily account for foals that had died or not made it to term. From the way she was behaving in anyone's presence, as well as her physical condition, it was pretty obvious she'd sustained prolonged and consistent neglect and mistreatment during her breeding life, only to end up in a slaughter yard along with her foal when deemed no longer useful.

Because Joleena was holding so much trauma in her body, we wondered if massage might help break down some of her barriers, providing of course we could get a hand on her to find out. I'd had such wonderful breakthroughs with Lincoln and Bowen therapy that I thought it was worth a go. I enlisted Alwyn's help in the afternoons when we went over to the five-acre paddock on my neighbour's property to feed the small herd grazing there.

On massaging Joleena, Alwyn says, 'I was pretty apprehensive. I was worried I would do it wrong because I had no experience massaging horses. But horses and people have a similar muscular system and both get tight and sore muscles in the same way. I put my hand on Joleena's neck and realised just how tight those muscles were. What was interesting the first time was that I tried to go too quickly up behind the ear but she didn't like me rushing her and turned to swing at me. So I had to back off pretty fast.

'Then I just laid my hand on her and left it there until she was fine with that and then just started going really slowly and gently. And it became blindingly clear to me that the problem was that I'd had a set outcome in mind, that I *had* to get to this muscle and get her to relax. But that was in conflict with her agenda, which was just to feel safe. It just didn't work.

'I was stressed about it, and she was picking up on my stress, so I just sort of blanked my mind for a moment and concentrated on being in that moment with her and connecting with her. Connection – that was the word that really popped into my head. After that, she started lowering her head and let me move my hand up to behind her ear again. I just felt really honoured that she let me do that. It was a high-stress environment to start with but then it became something really beautiful.'

Alwyn started to observe the complexities that exist between a therapist and a client, and how this would affect the progress of a treatment.

'Sometimes, I come into hospital, for example, and someone will tell me that a patient is difficult or abusive or has lashed out, but I often find it's a simple case of letting go of any kind of expectation about them and just being with them at eye level. If you're towering over them, then you've got power over them and they start acting a certain way. That's a really good example of the predator–prey relationship therapists can have with patients, and working with rescue horses made me realise it.

'It's very important when you come in with a client or a rescue horse that you're in partnership, and then you really can connect. If you are focused on the outcome, then you'll do whatever you can to achieve that outcome regardless of the consequences. But if you are focused on just connecting and letting the process unfold and take care of itself, then you're in partnership.'

When it came to Joleena's rehabilitation, this outcomes-based approach was something I spent long hours thinking about and discussing with others. Joleena was, without a shadow of doubt, the most complicated and challenging behavioural rescue we did. I called in numerous professionals, purported horse whisperers, to help Joleena. But as her towering walls remained resolutely firm, they became frustrated and either lost interest or, worse, began to resort to punishment and bullying to get what they wanted, even hitting her, which only compounded the problems.

From my perspective, the biggest problem for me as a manager of her rehabilitation was not that Joleena was going to be near impossible to rehome as she was. My biggest concern was ultimately her welfare. In my mind, I *had* to be able to get her to a place where she was able to have her hooves maintained safely and easily enough that a farrier would take on the job without fear of being hurt and without anger at the amount of time it took to do it. After all, it isn't a farrier's primary job to train a horse. To expect them to work on a horse whose feet *you* can't pick up is ridiculous. The constant tension was that if she developed a hoof condition that did require intensive treatment, we simply wouldn't be able to do it. The bottom line, I thought, was that even wild zoo animals are trained to participate in a level of medical care, so surely our horses should as well.

But the flipside to this was always the question of whether or not these two mares would be better off going to live out their lives as wild horses in a situation where, ultimately, they took the same risks as any wild horse. And that meant potentially harrowing injuries and illnesses that went untended and death that would eventually come, perhaps violently or with long, suffering torment. It was natural, certainly. But nature isn't always kind. Surely, I reasoned with myself in the middle of the night, it was better if we could help her get to the stage of trusting people just enough to be able to attend to her physical needs?

That was my outcome. But it wasn't Joleena's.

When the mares first arrived into the care of our charity, they spent about five months at a foster location while they put on weight, had some basic veterinary care where it could be managed with sedation, and weaned their beautiful foals, who both found wonderful homes. Then the mares came to foster with me and Alwyn at our home for seven months, and we began to explore different ways to break through their behavioural challenges, with little success. As fortune's fate would have it, I was contacted by a pair of young women who had been training in the Parelli system of horse communication for many years and were steadily working their way up the levels of qualified trainers. They offered their services free of charge if we would like it. Well, did I have a case for them!

So the mares left our place to go to another foster location, for around nine months, where the Parelli trainers could access them more easily. Their agenda, while taking into account my wishes for the ability to handle their feet, was far greater and more comprehensive in scope. Their focus was not merely on achieving an outcome but on establishing a relationship with the horses so they were able to *welcome* attention to their hooves.

It was through the Parelli system of equine communication that I learned about the three states of prisoner, prey and partnership in a horse. It was something I'd read about but never fully explored, never having had to deal with a behaviourally challenging horse before I started a horse rescue organisation.

If a horse is in the state of prisoner, it is forced to act, and may be restrained, punished, or rewarded for various behaviours. In this state, the horse may be compliant but has actually given up or gone dead inside. (A lot of riding school horses would fall into this category.) The horse in a state of prey might be fearful of authority, locked into the flight/freeze/fight way of thinking, or feel constantly pursued if it sets a boundary but the human ignores it. (A lot of horses described as 'crazy' or 'dangerous' would fall into this category.) But a horse acting in partnership with a human willingly participates, feels free to express itself without recriminations, is internally motivated (perhaps by curiosity or joy) and shares open communication with the human. This, of course, is what we all want with our horses. And this is what the Parelli trainers set out to achieve: a state which would naturally lead to the mares' participation in hoof trimming because they *wanted* to, not because they *had* to.

I was never a robust practitioner of Parelli but I did love the philosophy and much of the reading I did, and watching the trainers in action was like watching a masterful ballet. Alwyn and I shared many discussions about the interrelationships between humans and horses, and practitioners and clients.

'I think all things go wrong with therapy when you're not connecting with your clients, because if you're in partnership with them, they'll naturally tell you what you need to be doing and you listen and respond to that.

'Therapists get into a healing profession because they want to help a client but sometimes they come across someone they think is difficult or not doing what they want them to do, and it's almost like they want to be in control of the situation, they want power over the situation. I can spot it a mile off now, after working with rescue horses, because I can have a client turn up who's had bad experiences with therapists in the past and they walk in the door and they actually look like a frightened horse, looking around and you can see them thinking, *I wonder if I can get out of here*, or they look apprehensive when you say you want to put your hands on them. And when you ask permission from them, which is essential when you're working with horses, you can see the client change. That's when you get into partnership with them.

'Of course, I'm not perfect. Sometimes things don't go well – we're only human so it's going to happen sometimes – just as it did when I first massaged Joleena. It's how you then choose to react to it that's important.

'You rarely find a client who fights you, though that does happen sometimes, especially in a hospital setting when you might have someone in extreme pain. They more often freeze, play dead, like *I'll just lie here and just not really answer questions*. I guess you find flight in a client who just doesn't come back. A lot of my day is spent with clients who've come to me because they've had a bad experience with other therapists where they never went back. That's a bit sad because that therapist never got that feedback so they'll never know why that person didn't return. And someone in flight is never going to go back to the person they're running from.'

Just like a horse would never go back to the lion stalking them.

The exceptional thing with horses is that, because of their size, their feedback is going to involve some sort of big gesture, something that could do you serious damage, something you can't ignore that tells you what you're doing isn't working. Alwyn and I discussed the idea of running horsemanship training workshops for therapists in client–therapist communication. Horses are large, in-your-face clients who can give very honest and specific feedback on how a therapist's approach is affecting them.

'If a therapist, for whatever reason – stress, frustration, time pressure – switches off that connection they could miss valuable information. The signs with people are very subtle – the little turn of the mouth or that little tension in their shoulders. It's always a non-verbal with people if they're not comfortable, just like it is in horses with flaring of the nostrils or stamping on the ground or swishing of the tail or something like that.'

In other words, the feedback is immediate.

'Very immediate and very powerful feedback. When I was working with Joleena, I had that apprehension of thinking I'd better learn fairly quickly how to do this because she is potentially a dangerous horse. The consequence for me was probably going to be more than just a client that may not come back. A client probably wouldn't kick me and injure me.'

Being in partnership with your horse means being in rapport, which is another concept so vitally important in healing professions. In any situation when a person who is sick or injured, or has mental health issues, ends up in a medical situation, there is a power imbalance there already because the patient doesn't necessarily have the resources right at that moment to stand up for themselves or get what they want, or even express themselves clearly.

'This really triggered a desire in me to learn more about the dynamics of communication. It's been proven that if doctors have rapport with their client, their accuracy in diagnosis rate improves. You just can't have rapport if you're in a metaphorical predator–prey relationship. So I suppose the challenge for therapists is that a person's in stress before they even come to our office. They're already in fight, flight or freeze.

'It's how you deal with that stress that's crucial. Are you okay with someone being stressed and do you even acknowledge it? Something they talk about in NLP (neuro-linguistic programming) is matching and mirroring – if someone's stressed and you're not aware of it, you'll start holding your breath or talking with clipped tones. If you can just regulate your own breathing, your client will start to match it.'

This type of mirroring is obvious with horses. If you approach a horse in a stressed state, or you've just had a fight with someone and you're angry, it's common for the horse to react strongly to the energy you're bringing to that situation. They become outward mirrors for your internal state. And it's this quality that makes them such powerful therapy assistance animals.

'Another rescue horse we had, Tansy, really taught me that. She had a tendon injury that I was doing ultrasound on. And I was rushed that day and I thought, *right, I've got ten minutes to do this treatment on her leg, I have to get out the door but I really have to do this treatment 'cause she's got this tendon injury and she really needs this treatment.*

'Well, she would not have a bar of me. She walked away from me, lifted her leg up, stamped her foot. She was giving me every clear signal possible that she did not want to be involved in a haphazard treatment. Again, it's been proven with people that if your client is aware that the doctor or therapist is rushed then they won't raise everything, they won't communicate what's going on because they don't want to disadvantage the doctor or the next client. They don't want to be a burden or they just don't feel comfortable being with someone who's rushing. Do you really want someone with a complex piece of equipment working on you if they're rushed? Even on a deeper biological level, if someone's rushing, then we think there must be something wrong.

'I think the thing that Joleena really taught me is that you don't have words so you just can't explain away a stressful situation. You have to use your actions and your mastery over your own internal state to work with a horse. And most communication is not words anyway, so it's a real asset to have those skills when working with clients.'

By the time the mares had finished up their time in their third foster home and working with Parelli, they'd been with our organisation for nearly two years. Our policy was that we would hold onto a horse for life rather than see it end up in the wrong hands. I used to wonder if those mares were going to spend the rest of their lives running around our backyard. Although there had been improvements, neither was ready to live with someone from the general public. They had progressed in their understanding of humans through highly trained and experienced Parelli hands, but as soon as anyone with less technical knowledge interacted with them they reverted immediately to their defensive and evasive behaviour. And their participation in hoof care was hit and miss. Just as they had the first day we met them, they still showed absolutely no interest in making a connection with people.

Other rescue horses we'd had, like Lincoln, were traumatised but still showed a strong desire to connect with people. But Joleena and her friend, Shona, had no such desire. I was sure that if they never saw another human again for as long as they lived they'd be happy with that. They also made no connections with other horses. They were each other's herd and that's the way they wanted it to stay.

I was pleased, however, with the change in the way it felt to be around Joleena. I no longer felt a sense of alarm just being near her. Her invisible barbed fortress was softer. She had most definitely released some of her fear and I was pleased for her own sake if nothing else.

Still, I was back to the same dilemma. Where did their future lie? And because the mares were so closely bonded, I didn't want to separate them, making it even harder to place them.

As so often happened to me when running a rescue charity, an amazing opportunity popped up. Gaye Harvey, who'd been supporting the charity since its inception, was from a place called Horse Heaven outside of Stanthorpe. She ran retirement facilities for horses on hundreds of acres and she said that both the mares were welcome to live out their days there, exactly as they were showing they wanted. They do have regular care, though. They still get their teeth done and they have farrier attention and worming and extra feed if they need it. In other words, they did indeed find themselves in their own equine heaven.

'They are still inseparable,' Gaye says. 'Where one goes, the other follows, and they are still very wary of strangers. When they had to have their Hendra vaccinations they would only let me give them to them. They aren't nasty, just standoffish and very capable of not being caught! I have given up trying to put halters on them; it seems to stress them more. I can always just hold a rope around their necks and they stand like angels. They enjoy their freedom. Even though they are with a big herd, they are always just off to the side, enjoying each other's company.'

I was most relieved for Joleena that she found a home with Gaye. Shona had the same problems but wasn't aggressive. Rather, she was more prone to flight reactions. But Joleena was a horse almost no one wanted to touch. She had taught us so much while she'd been with us and now she could move on and live her life out peacefully, free of the burdens and stresses humans had once caused her. She'd chosen to retreat from the human world and I had come to terms with that. I hadn't been able to rescue her in the way I wanted to (to help her become a relaxed, people-loving horse) but she'd found her place, as free and natural as possible, spending days with her best friend. And she'd passed on some valuable lessons to Alwyn in the process, ideas that now inspire his daily work.

'Before I was involved with horses, I saw them around but I'd never connected with them. But then I learned to see them in a whole new way. And what I started to feel, especially once we started taking in rescues, was such sadness for the history of horses and all they'd done for humankind over the centuries. They were this noble, important, valued member of society and now, because of industrialisation, they don't have that same place any more so their perceived inherent value is so much less, and only demonstrable by making money racing or breeding or the like.

'What the rescues have taught me, especially ones like Joleena, is that they still have this really important contribution to make to society. It struck me one day that horses used to help us with transport and opening up the country. They helped us get to places much faster than we ever could without them. And I realised they still can help us get there – mentally and emotionally – faster than we could get there ourselves. I had a lot of ideas about patient–therapist relationships before we started rescuing horses but Joleena helped me formulate those philosophies much faster than I could ever have done without her in my life.'

PHANTOM

Eleisha Ifield stood in the horse yard, waiting.

The horse dealer walked towards the big grey gelding he described as dangerous, unpredictable, flighty and difficult – a horse marked for slaughter but one he told Eleisha she could save for eight hundred dollars if she was game.

He carried a saddle and tossed it on the horse's back. He yanked the girth strap and the horse reared straight up in the air and threw himself backwards, landing on a timber bench, smashing it to pieces and taking out the corner of a shed in the process. The horse got back to his feet, shaking all over, a lather of terrified sweat, a bleeding cut on his shoulder, his eyes like saucers.

A shocked silence. Then the horse dealer dropped the price by half.

Eleisha hadn't been looking for a horse. In fact, at that time in her life she wasn't really looking for anything other than to survive each day. The only constant in her life, the only thing that still brought her any joy, was horses – a passion shared by her mum and her older sister, Rachel.

'I was out riding with Rachel that day. We were having a heart-to-heart as I was in the throes of a very messy divorce, leaving behind a horrible marriage that had left me scarred. I trusted no one, had no self-esteem or self-worth and was very unwell.

'Along the way we passed a neighbour's property, and he happens to be a horse dealer. Standing in his paddock I saw a stunning grey head poking out from a hessian combo rug, beautiful ears pricked in our direction. And I fell in love. Instantly. Just like that.'

Doubtful she'd be able to afford such a beautiful horse, but driven by a powerful attraction, Eleisha went to speak to the dealer anyway.

Phantom was marked for disposal to the local dogger in a few days' time. The dealer told Eleisha he was sick of dealing with the horse, that he was dangerous and difficult and too much trouble, but said she could buy him if she wanted.

'It broke my heart,' Eleisha says. 'I've always been a horse lover and believe no horse should be dogged. No horse should be disregarded because of the damage *we* have caused to *them*. I decided I would try him out and see just how dangerous he was.'

She went back the next day to ride him and when she arrived, Phantom was without a rug, showing his notable Thoroughbred breeding and shining dark-grey coat.

'He was beautiful. My heart just melted. He was the horse you dream of as a little girl. A stunning Barbie horse. Pretty and perfect. The most divine-looking horse I'd ever seen.'

Anxious to meet her potential new mount, Eleisha got out of the car and walked straight over. But as she approached him, every muscle in his body tensed, his eyes widened to show the whites, and he pulled backwards on the rope as far as he could go, putting as much distance as possible between himself and Eleisha.

'I knew something bad had happened in his life but there was more there than that. There was something in his eyes. Even then I could see that if I could get past the trust issue he would be great. He wanted to trust. He wanted to get past the fear and bond with someone.'

When the dealer brought out the saddle, Phantom 'just lost his mind'. Still, despite the extreme display he put on, rearing and smashing the bench, she believed she had to get him out of that environment.

The dealer lunged him in circles on a long rope to try and burn off some of Phantom's energy to make him easier for Eleisha to ride. But that was yet another chance for Phantom to display his issues and he bucked 'like a machine' the whole time.

Finally, serious doubts began to form. But despite everything she'd seen that morning, everything the dealer had told her about him throwing people off over and over again and the inner voice telling her she couldn't do it, she got on the horse.

'And he was the most beautiful, light, responsive horse I'd ever ridden. Admittedly, he was knackered from being lunged, but he was just divine. So sensitive.'

What on earth made her get on him?

'Balls of steel!'

She can laugh about it now, but that moment might have been tragic. Instead, it was brave and changed her life forever.

'Seriously, I don't know why I got on him. He was stunning. And all I kept thinking was that I'd ridden difficult horses before and there was something more inside him. It was the look in his eye. I knew this wasn't truly him; this wasn't what he wanted to be. I wanted to save him. I wanted to help him. I was coming out of a divorce and I was damaged and scarred and *I* was frightened of everything that came near me as well and I probably saw a little bit of myself in him.' She pauses, shrugs. Laughs. 'And he was pretty.'

Because Phantom had been nice to ride, the dealer put the price back up to six hundred dollars, and Eleisha accepted. The dealer's final words were, 'If he breaks your arm, I don't want to know about it. Get rid of him yourself. I don't want him back.'

Eleisha grew up in Mount Walker, the youngest of five siblings, with her mum as the single parent.

'I got married very young, not quite twenty-three, and he was not quite thirty-three. It wasn't the most healthy relationship. We got together when I was eighteen and we separated when I was twenty-five. I was way too young for that relationship and I couldn't recognise what was right for me. I'll preface everything by saying that I don't think he was a bad person, we just weren't right for each other.'

Eleisha's first husband had just come out of a divorce when they met. He had no children from the first marriage and Eleisha told him she wasn't sure she would ever want any of her own. He said he was fine with that but Eleisha says it all changed after they got married.

'Everything he loved about me in the beginning was everything he hated about me in the end. I ate wrong – I was too noisy, the cutlery on the plate was too noisy; I sneezed too much, coughed too much, laughed too loudly; when I was in a group, I didn't talk to the whole group, I concentrated on one person, and I should be making eye contact with everybody. He would kick me under the table. I would get dressed at home and he would tell me I looked beautiful but then we'd go out and he'd ask me why I always dressed like a slut. Then it was my weight – he'd tell me I had a big arse.

'By the time we separated I was pretty damaged. I had an eating disorder and no sense of self-worth. When you're with someone who's supposed to love you unconditionally and they tell you everything about you is wrong . . . I can't believe I'm crying . . . you start to doubt everything about yourself and who you are and the decisions you make. Even to the point where I questioned if separating and leaving was the right decision. I had no faith in myself whatsoever.

'The eating disorder came about from control because the only thing I could control in my relationship was what I ate.'

Eleisha's husband always did all the cooking. Every time he put food down in front of her, she only ate half of whatever was there. In response, her husband kept putting less and less food on the plate. But no matter what amount of food was there, Eleisha only ate half of it, until she was barely eating at all.

'It didn't start from weight. Not at all. It was literally about me being able to control the one thing he couldn't control. I don't know why half. It was just something I decided in my head.

'I had no control over money, where I went or who I saw. He

separated me from my family. It got to the point where I was a shell of myself. No confidence. No strength. No happiness or joy in my life. Horses were my only escape; they always have been. The one time I felt *right* within myself was when I was with the horses. It was the one constant. The one thing I never wavered on, including in that relationship. He used to get very resentful of the horses and the time I spent with them.'

At that time, Eleisha had Major, a beloved horse with whom she did western pleasure. 'Major is a national champion western pleasure horse, but we got bored of that and tried pony club. We did one gymkhana and he was a superstar. He cleaned up.'

But it was only when she was with Major that she was happy.

'I'm not the kind of person who would take their own life. But I didn't see much value in life any more. The only thing I had was the horses and two dogs that relied on me to look after them.

'I started to see a psychologist through work and she said to me, "You know what you want to do and you only have enough of yourself left to do it. And you need to do it." And that's when I made the decision to ask him to move out.

'Then living on my own, things got really bad. I kept not eating but now it was justified by money. I wanted to prove that I could take care of myself and run my own life. But I had to feed two horses and two dogs and they came first. I paid the mortgage, I had to get to work by bus, and whatever was left, which was nothing, was food. I ate popcorn and crackers.

'I laugh about it now because if you don't laugh you cry.'

Eleisha's family knew something was wrong, but she had become very good at hiding it and fobbing off their concerns. And because such a separation from her family had been established in the marriage, the only time they saw her was when she was with her horses – and when she was with her horses was when she was happy.

In the end, she lost nearly 20 per cent of her body weight. 'I was borderline hospitalisation. I wasn't hungry. I was past it. I would have a sorbet juice drink for lunch and a little microwave popcorn for dinner. But I still didn't believe I had a problem.'

Rachel, Eleisha's sister and best friend, says, 'She looked terrible. Terrible! I was worried about her because she said she was fine and there was no real talking to her about it. I even threatened to admit her to hospital. All I could do was support her as best I could and be there for her when she asked.'

'I used to go to the gym and I'd weigh myself when I started and if I hadn't lost weight by the time I finished I'd make myself go back and do more,' Eleisha says. 'I got it in my head that I had to consume fewer calories in a day than I could burn on a treadmill, which was about three hundred and fifty calories. I got a sense of satisfaction from losing weight but it was all about control. It was all about that number being mine to control.'

Today, Eleisha has a very healthy, fit physique, one many women would envy.

'Now I eat whatever the hell I want.'

Contributing to Eleisha's sadness was the forced retirement of her superstar horse, Major, due to navicular syndrome (inflammation and degeneration of the navicular bone in the front feet, associated with significant lameness). The world was closing in around her.

Rachel took her riding. And that's when Eleisha stumbled across Phantom.

'Initially, Phantom was such a massive distraction – a project. That was such a ray of hope in my life. Another horse person will understand that when you're with your horse, nothing comes into it, nothing distracts you, nothing changes your mood. You're just so consumed by what's going on in that moment that the world could explode around you and you're happy on your horse. You get that partnership and that connection. He was my everything. He was my confidante, my distraction, my love. I could see he loved me as much as I loved him. And he loved me for who I was. He didn't give a crap if I hadn't brushed my hair, had no makeup on, wore dirty tracksuit pants. Animals love you for who you are, not for what you look like or what you can give them.

'As the extent of Phantom's damage started to become evident, I started to reflect on myself and my own damage, and his responses began to mirror my responses. He taught me patience. He also taught me about communication. If I didn't ask Phantom to do something the right way, he would take off, kick, rear, strike or run away. I started to really learn that you don't have to accept being treated like crap. You can say no, and unless you're going to treat me properly, then you go over there and I'll go over here, thanks very much.

'Phantom was really the *journey* . . .' She pauses and drops her head in her hands. 'Oh my God. I *hate* that word. I feel like I'm on *Australian Idol* right now.' She takes on a mock reality television show voice. 'It's my *journey*. I have a *journey*. Do you want to hear about my *journey*?

'But seriously, Phantom was the start of me learning how to show people how I wanted to be treated and only allowing people into my life who are going to treat me right. And educating those who are in my life who don't treat me right in how to do that. And we all have choices. Everything is about choices. You can't change people; all you can do is change your choices. You choose to accept a person's behaviour or you choose to walk away from that person. If you choose to walk away, that person then has a choice to change their behaviour or walk away. And if you can't walk away, you have a choice of how to handle that. I try to live that every day.'

She suppresses a smirk and the mock reality television voice returns. 'So my word for this interview will be *choice*.'

Phantom taught Eleisha she could be strong and confident again.

'He taught me that I was capable of helping someone else and that meant I must have been strong. And he taught me I was capable of something bigger than myself and bigger than the failure of a relationship, which in the scheme of things is such a non-event. I mean, the stuff that people go through in life . . . to be messed up by someone giving you a hard time for while . . . I know I'm trivialising what I went through but it's a big wide world and there's a lot of bad stuff out there. You've just got to learn to grow and not be a victim. And Phantom's taught me a lot of that.'

Eventing and competitions might be Eleisha's passion, but Phantom isn't what most would consider the ideal eventing horse. There was a lot to work through with him when he arrived, and seven years later there still is, though obviously much less.

'I think it will be something I'm doing for the rest of his life, because I owe it to him.'

Eleisha's plan in the beginning was to take as much pressure off Phantom as possible. She would saddle him up and take him out casually, just letting him get the feel of his surroundings and get to know her. But even that was enough to tip him over every time.

'He'd just plant his head down and buck and bolt. So much fear. And probably, in hindsight, there was a lot of pain there as well. I probably should have done more physio with him. There was obviously something else going on that was more than the fear, because the bucking was pretty profuse. And then I started reading about damaged horses and how to handle them and I got onto a natural horsemanship book and read that and it seemed to make sense.

'You can project a lot of human emotions on horses but I really believe he knew I was there to help and make his life better. It was my main goal that he would never see a day of fear again in his whole life.'

And with that at the forefront of everything she did with him, the walls slowly started to break down.

'I only read one book and it would make me a bit of an idiot to think I know anything about natural horsemanship, but whatever we've been doing has clearly worked because he's an entirely different horse now. You couldn't walk up to him in the beginning. Now he walks up to you. He wasn't dangerous; he was scared. And there's a big difference in a horse between dangerous and scared.'

Other than the fact that Phantom can be a particularly difficult

The author, Joanne, and her much-loved horse Lincoln
Courtesy of Kathleen Lamarque

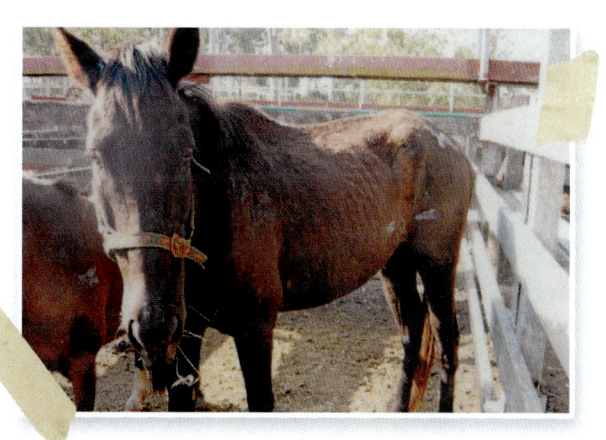

Lincoln, waiting in the auction pen
Courtesy of the author

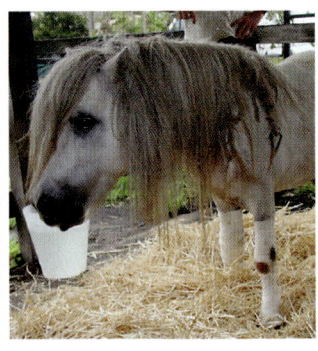

Elf in hospital after his attack
Courtesy of the RSPCA Queensland

Elf
Courtesy of Jane Crutchfield

Elf meets the author's husband, Alwyn, and their son, Flynn
Courtesy of the author

Elf in his new home, with endless opportunities ahead
Courtesy of Jane Crutchfield

Groover, hanging out at home at the back door
Photos courtesy of Vicki Morrow

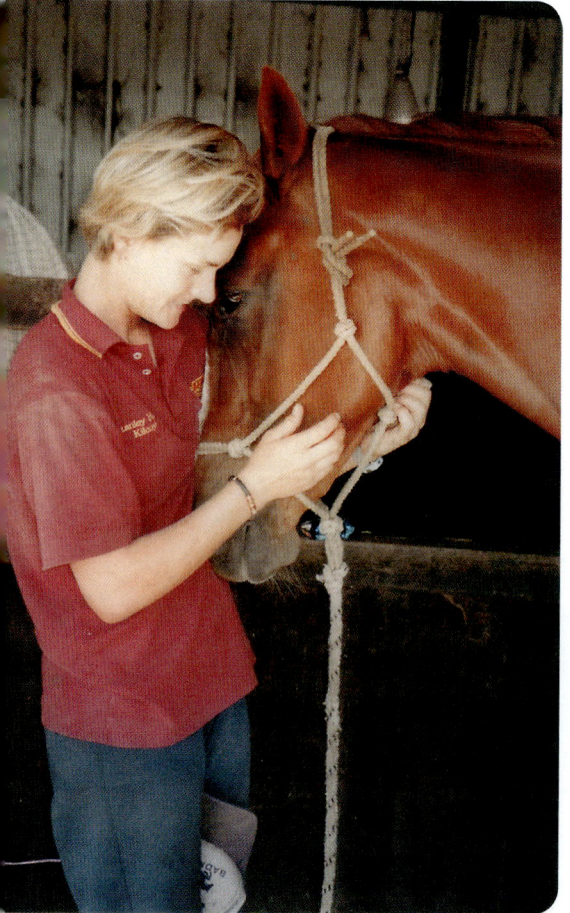

Rebel and Groover

Soul, after being rescued from his fall down the cliff
Courtesy of Beverly Finnigan

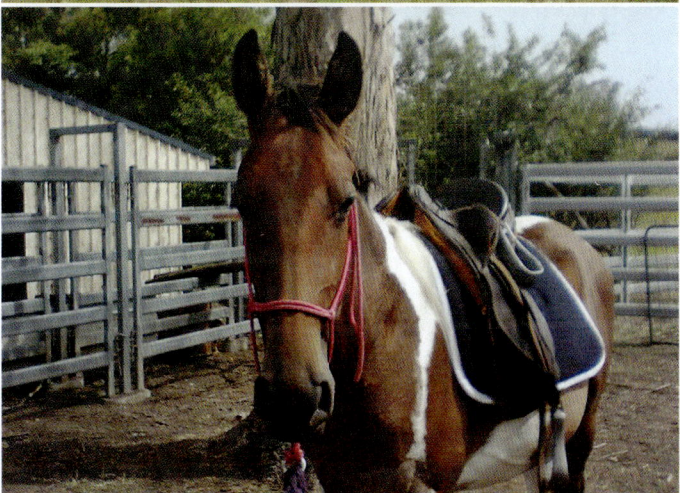

Soul, now in training
Courtesy of Kelsie Consadine

Dallas and Olivia, best friends forever
Courtesy of the author

Dallas, seized by the RSPCA
Courtesy of Carrie Palmer, with permission of RSPCA Tasmania

Dallas's new home, high above the Tamar River
Courtesy of the author

Michael working with Ruben in the round yard at Horses for Hope
Photos courtesy of Horses for Hope

Michael and Belle

Joleena and her best friend, Shona, retired for life at Horse Heaven
Courtesy of Gaye Harvey

Joleena
Courtesy of Carly-Jade Haora

Eleisha and Phantom sharing quiet time
Courtesy of Gavin Ifield

Eleisha and Phantom competing together
Courtesy of Mandy Smith

Astro and Nicole, waiting for help
Photos courtesy of Peter Ristevski/Newspix

Free at last

The working donkeys of Egypt
Courtesy of Jacqui and Brett Steele

Jacqui with her beloved donkeys, at home at Big Ears Animal Sanctuary
Courtesy of the author

Boo and Jennah
Photos courtesy of Rebecca Larosa

Boo, regaining trust and confidence

Larry and Sue
Courtesy of Brooke Avery from Sun Dust Summer Photography

Salty, following Scilla's granddaughter, Poppy, around the arena
Courtesy of Scilla Sayer

Salty, attending Scilla's mother's memorial service
Courtesy of Tess Jenkin

Salty
Courtesy of Scilla Sayer

horse to train or take out because of his anxiety and reactions to circumstances and events, he won't jump anything higher than eighty centimetres, which is the introductory level of eventing. The next step up is ninety-five centimetres.

'It's a big step up to ninety-five. But he's a water baby and he'll jump a one-star water jump (the first rung of the International Federation of Equestrian Sports certification), just because he loves water and will jump into anything in water.'

'I'd love to ride professionally but I'm very much a weekend warrior. I don't have the time to spend that I'd like in order to progress to professional levels. I took up eventing quite late. We've learned together. I've gone to a lot of clinics. I don't know if I could ever be professional. I think there are certain choices you need to make at that level that I'm not prepared to make. Because for me, deep down, my theory with Phantom and with all horses going forward from here is that I will do as much as they want to do. He jumps eighty centimetres and I barely have to ask. I will never wear spurs on him. I won't carry a whip. I won't force him into a situation that he doesn't want to put himself into.

'I took him to a clinic once and he was refusing a water jump so I should have known there was something wrong. The instructor asked me to try again but he backed out at the last minute. And the instructor told me to grab a crop. And I said no, I wouldn't carry one. But he said it again. And I am so cranky with myself for this, but I took the crop. He told me to hit him with it. I tapped Phantom on the shoulder and the instructor told me to hit him properly. I told him that I didn't want to hit him harder, but he said if you're going to do it, do it properly. I hit Phantom the same way again and cantered him around to face the jump again and he stopped. The instructor told me to hit him again. I looked down and Phantom was shaking all over like a leaf.

'I told the instructor enough was enough, that we'd already pushed way beyond what either of us was comfortable with and I handed him back his crop. I took Phantom to a different spot and popped him over a smaller jump and he went over perfectly. In his mind, there was something wrong with that water jump and I should have respected that because it was something we weren't capable of doing.

'And I will never make that mistake again. I will never let myself be coerced into that sort of riding when I know it's wrong. It's not that Phantom's not capable of jumping higher than eighty centimetres; he can and has jumped over a metre. But it's a particular shape of jump that he just doesn't have the confidence in himself for. I don't want to take the fun out of it for either of us. He hits jumps that he's not confident in, and that's dangerous for him and for me. It's not fair. He's given me so much of himself, trust-wise, that it's nasty of me to ask because he will try and he will hurt himself. We have a ball every time we go out. Especially now that we've worked through so much. And that's enough for me.

'Personally, I think that should be the philosophy across all equestrian events. If a horse wants to gallop around the racetrack, great – look at Phar Lap or Black Caviar. They *want* to run. If they don't want to jump, why make them?'

Eleisha bought her latest equine friend, Toby, in the hope that he will jump higher than eighty centimetres and be able to progress through eventing levels.

'But I love Toby so much. And if he decides he doesn't want to compete in eventing, then we'll find something else. But he's my baby. He's not going anywhere.'

The bond between Eleisha and Phantom is indisputable. Just standing in the paddock for a few moments is enough to see how strong their relationship is. She calls him by clicking her tongue in a way that's almost like a chatting mother bird and he comes from wherever he is in the paddock. His eyes are focused solely on her. He relaxes under her hands. When she brushes and saddles him, he stands where he is with no halter and no ropes, completely calm.

Eleisha keeps things simple and rides in a snaffle bit and bridle and saddle, nothing else. And when they ride, Phantom transforms from a horse lazing around a paddock into a truly willing and engaged partner – one that listens to every single movement of her hands, seat and legs. His energy picks up and he rounds and softens into dressage moves, his hooves floating across the green grass. He radiates true pleasure. His ears flick back and forward in an attentive way, anticipating what Eleisha will ask him next. There's no resistance in his movements at all. It's like he's been waiting his whole life for her. If that sounds romantic, it's because it is. They are poetry in motion.

Rachel says, 'Eleisha's patience with horses is incredible and she works with them to reach mutual understanding. Phantom and Leish were both broken souls that found each other. He taught her to see the good in things when no one else could. He rewarded her for her kindness by being so giving in his responses and they formed an unbreakable, trusting partnership – which was something that had been lacking for both of them.'

Now still only fifteen years old, Phantom has grown into an accomplished eventing horse. But he still 'pigroots' in nearly every ride and will still buck from time to time, sometimes once or twice in a ride and sometimes in every second stride. Eleisha's well aware of his capabilities and limitations.

'I don't look at him through rose-coloured glasses. I look at him through opaque, practically discoloured, blind glasses.'

Ironically, as much as he plays up in general, Phantom has only ever once bucked during a dressage competition.

'He would pigroot a lot during a warm-up. And it got to the stage earlier this year where he would be pigrooting at a walk. I got physiotherapy, chiropractic and Bowen therapy done and everyone agreed there was nothing structurally wrong. So I think it was an anxiety thing.'

Despite Phantom's behaviour during competitions, he still manages to win or place highly at most events he enters. But it isn't about the winning for Eleisha; it's about the fun and the joy. And Phantom has brought her much joy. So, too, has her second husband, Steve.

'Phantom's my first guardian angel and Steve's my second. He's a saint. I've never met a better person. They were both sent to save me, that's for sure, because I was on a bad path.'

Eleisha met Steve at her sister's house after the separation from her husband and thought 'he was nice'. After three months, she knew he was the one for her. 'But I wouldn't let him ask me to marry him for five years because I didn't want to make a mistake. I was with my first husband for four years before we got married and you'd think I'd have known him. But I didn't.'

When they did get married, Eleisha rode Phantom down the aisle in her wedding dress and her sister escorted her on her own horse, while Steve rode a tractor. And Phantom behaved like the perfect gentleman.

Life is good for Eleisha now and she finds it difficult to look back and analyse how it had all gone so wrong before she met Phantom.

'The anorexia was a direct result of the situation I was in. After that situation was removed, I got happy and I got better. It wasn't immediate because I went through a bit of a gym addiction. But it all got better and I just got really, really happy.

'I look back and I wonder how this person I am now was ever in that situation. Back then, when I looked in the mirror, it wasn't like I saw a fat person. It was never that. I saw someone who could control her life, which was ironic because I couldn't. I didn't like myself. Now I look in the mirror and I see that I'm learning to be happy with the person I've become. It's not about what's on the outside, it's about the person you are and how you treat others and fit into the world. I've lost the desire to control the outside.

'I'm so content now. Maybe it's because Steve is so wonderful at loving me for me and that's teaching me how to do it. A lot of strength has come from knowing I'm a good person and when I touch people's lives I leave a positive mark rather than a pretty image. It's more important to have a good heart.

'I wouldn't change marrying my first husband because it's made me who I am and made me appreciate what I've got with Steve and good friends. I can recognise goodness in people a lot more easily than I used to.'

And in part, that has to do with her experiences with Phantom and seeing the goodness in a horse that everyone else had given up on.

'There was something there that needed to be nurtured and I just wanted to make his life better. He was making life hard for himself and for me but that just meant he was struggling with the process. I don't give up on lost causes. I feel very connected to him on another level, other than horse and rider. It broke me when he had to have ten months off with injury. I turned him out at my mum's place and the whole time I felt something was missing. I just want him to see that life's okay now. He doesn't need to fight or struggle because no matter what he throws at me, I'll still be there. He is still damaged and can still be very unpredictable. But then, scratch the surface and aren't we all?'

Possibly. But these two souls are partners, getting better together, each and every day, best friends for life.

ASTRO

In February 2011, Nicole Graham's beach ride at Geelong turned to near tragedy when her horse, Astro, got stuck in the mud and had to be rescued by teams of State Emergency Service (SES) and Country Fire Authority (CFA) volunteers.

The remarkable thing about Astro's story is not even that he *was* rescued but the fact that he made it out in spite of the *way* he was rescued. It could have all gone so terribly, terribly wrong for both Nicole and Astro. And it's because of this that Astro has become such an important figure in the world of Large Animal Rescue training.

Nicole's life revolves around horses. She's an equine dentist by trade, attends horse shows every weekend, breeds horses in a small way for her own collection, and has thirteen horses, distributed between her twelve acres in Lara, near Geelong in Victoria, and her mother's property nearby.

Before becoming an equine dentist, Nicole was a human prosthesis dentist.

'My career has always been in dentistry, and yet I basically ruined a really good horse by not getting his teeth done properly. Then at Equitana one year I discovered Ian Wharton and Whole Mouth Dentistry and found my passion for equine dentistry. I studied two years at Gunnedah with master dentists Ian Wharton and Zoe Swain. They're pioneers in the field and brought it to Australia.

'Even though I've always had horses and I'm a fourth-generation horse person, I only ever got someone to come and rasp their teeth. But after studying it, now I realise it's a real science. I concentrate on balancing through the jaw and the two sets of horses' teeth, and working on the whole head.'

These days, Nicole competes mostly in dressage events. She has three children who are all into horses and her nine-year-old daughter, Paris, is an avid show competitor. Her herd is made up of riding ponies, Warmbloods and Astro, a nineteen-year-old riding pony crossed with a Thoroughbred.

'Astro is a remarkable horse. I'm his third owner and he's taken my three kids to the absolute top with their riding and he was there for me to do my Equestrian Australia schooling so I could complete my instructor course. He is blind in his right eye and he has some peculiar habits but he's an absolute schoolmaster. He's got the best work ethic. And he's totally and utterly controlled by his stomach – sugar, carrots, apples, pears, bread, jam sandwiches . . . he does anything for a reward.

'He's cherry bay in colour, stands at 14.2 hands high and was a purpose-bred show Galloway. He's had a huge show career and his performance cards are outstanding. He's done Melbourne

Royal, Adelaide Royal, Sydney Royal, Grand Nationals and his most recent specialty is interschool competitions. He's an ordinary moving horse but he's such a working horse and he puts on the energy in the show ring. He quite often likes to put himself in first place in the line-up for a ribbon. He jumps extremely well. He's one of those horses you read about but you don't often see. He's only needed a vet three times in his life.'

When Nicole's youngest daughter, Paris, fell off her Shetland pony as a four year old and lost her confidence, Nicole decided to put her on Astro to get her confidence back.

'It was quite comical to see this tiny little child on this big pony but Astro was perfect for her.'

On the day of the rescue, Nicole and Paris went down to Avalon Beach to ride. There are racing stables nearby and the beach is a well-known 'horse beach', with jockeys taking racehorses down for track work. And Nicole says she's lived in the area her whole life and used to ride on the beach as a kid. So there was nothing unusual in what she was doing.

'It was about 36 degrees and we'd just finished a big competitive weekend and all Paris wanted to do was swim at the beach with the horses and the dogs. We loaded Astro and Emily – Paris's riding pony – on the float, along with the three dogs, and we went off to Avalon Beach.

'We got out of the car and got organised and Paris and I headed out to the water on our horses, and the blue heeler, Ringo, and the two chihuahuas came too. We went out into the water until the horses were about chest deep and then we decided to go parallel to the shoreline. We were probably about half a kilometre away from the car at this stage. Ringo sank first and then Emily went down.

I jumped off Astro and Paris jumped off Emily and Emily leapt her way out of the mud. Ringo did the same thing. I was helping them and Astro was just standing there – he's fairly economical like that.

'Once they got to the shore, I went back to Astro and took him by the bridle and turned to head back to shore but we were right on the edge of where they'd just dredged a channel for the salt-works, which is about a kilometre down the round. It creates little dams and ridges and turns it all into a big, sloppy bog – sticky, sticky mud. And when I turned him, we basically went straight into the dredging channel. After we sunk a bit, my feet found a pipe to stand on, so I felt safe at that time. But Paris was panicking a bit by this stage so I asked her to run back to the phone and ring my friend, Tess, and ask her to bring down a shovel and help me get out. At that stage I didn't really think we were in any drama.

'As it turns out, there are three Avalon beaches and Paris didn't know which was which and, honestly, I didn't realise that either; I just thought the horse beach was the horse beach. They've fixed that now and put up signs to say which beach is which. Paris came back and there was a couple walking down the beach with their dog so they came over and started to comfort Paris because she was starting to get a bit stressed. She tied Emily up to one of the plants on a sand dune and the dogs just sat on the mud, waiting. So we were all sort of stressed but quiet. The lady on the beach thought we'd need more than a shovel, so she helped Paris ring 000 and after about ten minutes the police turned up. They tried to walk on the mud and they sank straight away so they put the call into the SES and then it was all action.'

MaryAnne Leighton is the author of *Equine Emergency Rescue: a guide to Large Animal Rescue* and is the Queensland

Horse Council director responsible for Large Animal Rescue education. Her book forms the course material for all Large Animal Rescue training in this country. She knows Nicole and Astro's story well and stresses how important it is to know what action to take right from the start to give the horse the best chance of an injury-free recovery.

'If you find your horse trapped in mud and you cannot lead him out or encourage him to self-rescue, you must treat the situation as an emergency,' she says. 'Call 000 immediately and tell the operator you need a rescue truck (not a hose truck) and a crew trained in Large Animal Rescue techniques. Then call a large animal or equine vet who will probably have to sedate the horse before emergency responders can rescue him safely, and then treat him once he is free.'

But at the time of Astro's rescue, Nicole hadn't completed training in Large Animal Rescue and neither had the SES or CFA teams who arrived to help. What played out during the three and a half hours of the rescue was probably the course of action many of us would take. It seems logical but in fact it's a highly dangerous route. But one of the biggest things going for this rescue was that Nicole was blessed with a totally compliant horse.

'Astro was still calm. He didn't struggle at all. He just stood there.'

Time ticked on.

Nicole says, 'Paris was waiting on the beach and I could yell out to her from where we were. By this stage, she was really upset – she was only seven years old and we couldn't get in contact with her dad or her sisters so that was making her panic. But my friend Tess had arrived to look after her, and she settled down a bit. All we could do was wait until the SES got there.

'The SES and firefighters arrived. The SES tried to come out on the mud and realised it couldn't happen because it was really, really sticky. In the end they got a heap of wooden boards and made a bridge out to us and a bridge around the left side of us, which is where the more stable mud was. First of all we had a go at getting fire hoses around Astro. The fire hoses are like a flat canvas so we knew they'd be relatively safe, as opposed to rope, which would have just caused injury. So we had a go at that and they tried to lift him. But that didn't work because as you went up, it was almost like the mud pulled you back down again. He had been standing in mud up to his chest, but after they tried to lift him he actually went down deeper.

'Next, we tried to get him to jump up,' Nicole says. 'Because he's so well schooled, Astro will jump when you say, "Up!" So we got some boards in under him to try to give him some purchase with his hooves so he could pull himself up. But when he went back down the front half of his body went down further so he was actually rump high. And then we couldn't get the chest back up. At that point it was starting to get a bit iffy.

'The SES called the university, which is about fifteen minutes up the road, and there's a zoo there as well. So the vet from the university went over to the zoo and borrowed a zebra harness that they use for transporting zebras and they brought that over.

'Once we had the harness it was a question of how to get him out,' Nicole says. 'A helicopter was flying over Avalon Beach on standby, and it was going to do the lift if necessary. I was quite horrified at the thought because I'm scared of them and they were going to lift him up in the air. Thankfully, it didn't happen.'

At one point, the emergency crews considered bringing in a crane but because it was so sandy there was no way they could use it.

'Once the vet came into it, she wanted to give him a general anaesthetic because if he was limp it would be easier to break the suction and pull him out. I was a bit worried about that as well. I got really worried about him getting an infection in the needle site, which is quite stupid, but I think I was just trying to find an excuse to have a panic.'

Nicole had actually kept her cool the whole time.

'So we decided to do the general anaesthetic. And the whole time we put the harness on and did everything with Astro he just stood there. They kept bringing out bottles of water. He likes a Coke better, but he was happy with the water. He was just fantastic. He didn't struggle.'

There was a moment, though, when Nicole's daughter was overwhelmed.

'Paris overheard a couple of conversations about how quickly the tide was coming in and the rescue team had a discussion about how if they couldn't get him out within a certain amount of time then the only option was euthanasing him, because that would save him from drowning. But they were going to try the helicopter before that. Euthanasia was the last option. But that's when she was getting the most upset. She was sunstruck, emotional, stressed.'

It wasn't until the next day that Nicole really processed the enormity of the danger.

'At the time of the rescue, I didn't think that we weren't going to get out because I just couldn't let myself imagine it. I didn't see it on television till the next day, but seeing it all and seeing the tide coming in behind us was really scary. That's when it hit me more. I was glad I didn't look behind me that day because that would have made me panic.'

Thankfully, the final leg of their journey was nearly done.

'About a kilometre down the road there's a couple of beach shacks and one of the old fellas there had a tractor that they use to launch boats in and out of the water. He'd seen all the commotion so he brought his tractor down to see what was happening and told us he'd actually participated in a few horse rescues here before, pulling horses out of the beach, and so he helped us do the rest.'

The whole time this rescue drama was going on, a photographer, who'd heard the news on the police scanner, had been taking photos. Those photos ended up on the news around the world and went viral on the internet. A television crew was also there.

'I wasn't paying too much attention to them. There were so many people on the beach and once Tess was there to look after Paris I was just concentrating on holding Astro's head and talking to him and apologising to him profusely for embarrassing him like that because he's a very regal horse and I thought he'd be horrified that he was on television covered in mud like that.

'After the anaesthetic was given and he was pulled free, it took about an hour and a half for him to wake up and be ready to go home and I went home with him in the float. I didn't want to leave him there alone.'

From the next day, Nicole saw herself everywhere in the media, wearing her swimsuit.

'I was mortified! But I mean, when you go to the beach, you

wear a bikini, don't you? But I wasn't really appropriately dressed to go on TV, if I'd had my choice.'

Nicole has received a lot of media coverage and attention since the rescue and she's worked hard to turn it into something that can have an even greater impact. A magazine offered her money for her story and she gratefully donated it back to the Victorian SES for their assistance.

'I'm happy to talk to people about it for free. I'd rather they learn, like I had to. As much as there was positive feedback, some of the Facebook feedback was so mean. Comments like, "Why is a forty year old wearing a bikini?" I mean, how rude!

'Before all this happened, I would never have thought of having all these strategies and ideas in my head but now, since I've completed the Large Animal Rescue training, I'm much more onto it.

'I'm more confident now, I think. I've talked about it often since then. There was a lot of media attention after it first happened and I've never been one to be able to speak in public like that, but I found I was able to talk to people about it because it has a happy ending. And everyone loves a happy ending. And now I appreciate Astro even more. It could have ended so differently. I'm lucky, very lucky.'

Remarkably, Astro had no significant injuries after his rescue. In fact, Nicole took him to compete in a show the very next weekend and he won supreme pony club horse. He had some grazing under his dock from the harness and several weeks of skin irritation.

'They dump a lot of aviation fluid at Avalon Beach before the planes land, so a lot of the mud had aviation fuel in it and both of us came out with a really yucky rash for about three weeks. He also lost hair on his face, which has grown back white. He used to have one little white star on his forehead but now he has a lot of white on his face.'

Nicole says there is no way she would ever sell Astro.

'I get asked all the time if I want to sell him or lease him out and I wouldn't do it. It was always like that but the accident's made it more so. He's one of those true once-in-a-lifetime horses. And since that day, no one else can catch him. Only me. No kids. I'm his mum. He knows he's it to me and I'm it to him.'

Astro is now in semi-retirement and teaching Nicole's niece and nephew to ride.

Nicole and the rescue teams probably did exactly as any of us would do if we hadn't had the specific training in large animal rescue, but their efforts were a success despite the techniques used. Astro was a calm horse, which aided the process, but MaryAnne says this is rare.

'Most horses trapped in mud are unpredictable and extremely dangerous because they fight strenuously to free themselves. That's why I stress to my students they must always treat a trapped horse as though it were a hazardous material – a dangerous object that may explode without warning. Nicole was lucky Astro remained relaxed during his rescue as she was in the most vulnerable position, on her knees at his head. If he'd exploded, she would not have been able to move quickly to a safe place and could have been seriously injured.

'The mud exerted a strong suction on Astro's feet and legs, the same thing that happens when people try to walk in mud while wearing gumboots. The most important thing, even if the horse is in only six inches of mud, is to release that strong suction, otherwise you can cause serious injuries to his joints or leg muscles or even pull off his hooves. Releasing the suction is simple. Once rescuers have applied wide rescue straps around a trapped horse, they should inject water around his feet and legs and under his body until they are able to pull him free.'

But at the time, those there to assist hadn't yet attended one of the Large Animal Rescue courses and continued to do what they felt was most logical. The use of the zebra harness was good in theory, but actually caused injury to Astro beneath his tail.

'All they needed were two wide straps – either five-metre 'rescue straps' with ropes for pulling, or they could have improvised and used fire hoses. They needed one strap around Astro's girth (behind his front legs) and the other around his flank (in front of his back legs). Then they could release the suction around his feet and legs and pull him sideways.'

And as for the helicopter, MaryAnne says that lifting a horse that way is extremely expensive (and Nicole would have had to pay for it) and very dangerous.

'It must only be carried out if the horse is suspended in an approved harness.'

For MaryAnne, the most important piece of information she wants you to know concerns the use of the tractor.

'One of the golden rules of rescuing large animals is *never* to pull with a tractor or other vehicle. Yes, it takes a lot of manpower to drag a horse from mud but if you're pulling by hand you can feel when things go wrong. If, for example, Astro had one of his legs caught in barbed wire or a tree root, the hauling team would feel resistance, stop pulling immediately and clear the obstacle. However, if you pull with a vehicle, by the time someone realises there's a problem, tells the driver to stop, the driver hears the command and reacts, you may have caused terrible injuries to the trapped animal. In this situation, they got away with using that tractor. Next time they may not be so lucky.'

It's easy to see why MaryAnne is so passionate about her training courses and educating rescue teams on the safest, most practical, and surprisingly simple, equipment needed to succeed. As well as reducing the risk of injury, proper rescue techniques exponentially cut the amount of time it takes to resolve an ordeal.

'It was a revelation to Nicole and the SES and CFA volunteers to learn they could have had Astro out in thirty minutes, instead of three and a half hours,' MaryAnne says.

Properly educated and equipped rescue teams would have access to a piece of curved stainless steel tubing called a Nikopoulos needle. The Nikopoulos needle acts like a suture needle.

'It guides wide rescue straps around the torso of a horse trapped in mud or water, significantly reducing the stress on the horse and the time taken for the rescue because rescuers are not struggling through the mud to manually manipulate straps around the horse's body.'

For Nicole, the greatest gift from Astro's drama on the beach is the chance for her to advocate for people to educate themselves about the safe and proper way to rescue horses. She has completed two courses in Large Animal Rescue since that day.

'I like to talk to people about that. I've done talks at pony clubs. I carry MaryAnne Leighton's book around and I've gotten quite a few pony clubs to purchase it. I do try to educate people about it. While we were getting rescued, there were two teenagers riding at the start at the beach. They watched and they just kept on riding while we were getting rescued. It could have happened to them. The council has put in new signs and fenced off that area so you can tell now not to go along near there.'

The fantastic photos captured on that day and the subsequent frenzy of media attention has given Astro an amazing opportunity to be a poster child for the rescue work. In fact, Astro attended the workshops with Nicole.

'A lot of the SES folks were cow people so they didn't know how to lead a horse. It was interesting for them to learn to do that. Astro was great. He was happy to have a piece of bread and then participate for another three hours. He was led around by people who were learning how to approach a horse and how to tie ropes. He was the poster child,' Nicole says. 'I took the photos from Astro's rescue to the course. People were amazed that I didn't lose the plot and didn't panic. I couldn't panic because he needed me and if you panic, they're going to panic. I just had to bite my tongue. I was crying a lot and apologising to him profusely but I just kept talking to him the whole time.

'It's given me and Astro a profile,' Nicole says. 'I like to talk to people about it. The best thing you can do is not panic and get the training so you know when to use a rope and when to wait ten or fifteen minutes to get a fire hose, who to call for help and so on. You've just got to relax and think logically. You can achieve anything if you can do that. That's my motto now.'

It's that very same motto that came to Nicole's aid again, in February 2014. Nicole hadn't been back to the beach to ride for three years. 'I kept saying to people that I didn't need to go back to the beach again. But I now know that I was avoiding it.'

Nicole's sister finally persuaded her to the beach after a long stretch of extreme heat, with days regularly reaching over 40 degrees. But it didn't go as Nicole expected. Once she was back at the scene of the rescue, she says she 'lost it'.

'I just froze. I fell apart. I was so scared and I didn't know why but my feelings were so strong that I spooked everyone else there too and all the horses freaked out and wouldn't go near the water.'

They left the beach. But once away from the scene, Nicole used her motto to relax and think logically.

'I knew there was a problem; I just didn't know what it was.'

So she took herself to a hypnotherapy session, followed by a session with a sports psychologist. The psychologist suggested that she had post-traumatic stress and he went back with her to the beach and worked with her to move through her fears and blocks.

'And I think Astro has post-traumatic stress as well,' she says. 'At pony club, he'd started to hesitate at water jumps, so much so that I just said he wasn't to do them any more. But I also know that he was picking up on my fears and they were influencing him. I was looking for every aspect of danger rather than looking for the fun. And now that I know what I was doing, I've stopped it. I've realised I'm more comfortable with some boundaries around me, rather than in completely open spaces. But for now at least I feel better in a saddle in the water.'

It's a credit to Nicole that her thirst for learning and working things out helped her through the legacy of that day on the beach. And through that willingness to seek answers, she and Astro have made it back into the water once more.

THE EGYPTIAN HORSES AND DONKEYS

'You can make a difference to the lives of animals right now. If you want it badly enough, you'll find a way to do it.'

That's the message Jacqui Steele wants you to know. It's a message from her heart that keeps her going each day while her body slowly says goodbye.

As far as picturesque landscapes and scenery goes, Tasmania's Northern Midlands has plenty to please as you drive your way along the tourist trails. World heritage–listed convict sites, historic towns and rolling green fields delight at every turn. And Big Ears Animal Sanctuary Inc. sits on top of blue-green hills with uninterrupted views in all directions across pastures dotted with white sheep and grazing cows, yellow flowers and hay bales drying in the sun. The roads wend past cute stone homes with chimneys puffing smoke, fields of racehorses and trees so old they're permanently bent in the direction of the winds. For most of us, these sights bring joy. But for Jacqui Steele and her husband, Brett, the hundreds of farm animals that surround their home at Big Ears are evidence of animals in jeopardy.

'Every spring we see a heap of new lambs and we just think, how many of them will be dead tomorrow, the weak or abandoned ones left by the farmers to perish because it's simply not worth their time or money to save them?' Brett says.

This might sound morbid, negative or critical. But Jacqui and Brett are custodians of hundreds of rescued animals, many of them the product of the farming industry. Every single day the pair are asked for help, receive more animals, are told of horror stories, euthanase loved creatures and work to care for the residents of their sanctuary. They are, understandably, overwhelmed with the misery and suffering out there. They see clearly what most people don't.

Brett says, 'I do enjoy watching the animal behaviours, especially the young animals in the fields like spring lambs and calves. I'm grateful Australia hasn't yet turned into the mega factory farm situation that dominates the United States agriculture industry. It is rare to see animals in fields in the US, as almost all their livestock is either confined in massive sheds or in massive feedlots. For the animals in the fields around us, I also can't help but think of the dark side to their "idyllic" existence. Unfortunately every animal you see will most likely spend its last hours squeezed onto a truck with other scared and distressed animals and taken to the slaughterhouse where they will smell the blood of their own kind and hear the cries of pain and the sounds of death. I would rather see a world without animals than have the current levels of slaughter and cruelty to animals.'

It's a difficult insight to have. But it's what makes Jacqui and Brett do what they do every day of the year regardless of the weather, their finances, their own personal ambitions or challenges.

An overseas trip in December 2003 called Jacqui to accept a mission to help animals for the rest of her life – literally. Jacqui's life's work of helping animals is both her legacy and the passion and focus that keeps her here with us for as long as possible.

'My oncologist said to me that whatever I'm doing out here at the farm, to get back out there and keep going because I shouldn't be as good as I am. He credits it to the work I do with the animals and the time I spend with them. There's definitely a connection there.'

The four hundred animals that now live safely on her and Brett's property in Longford, Tasmania, owe their welfare to the Egyptian donkeys and horses the couple couldn't save back then.

One of the hardest things to come to terms with as a rescuer may be that despite all your best efforts you can never save every single animal. Suffering, trauma, pain and death will continue. The question then becomes, what do you do with all that grief, anger and frustration? What do you do to make the unbearable bearable? For Jacqui and Brett, the only answer was to take action. The result is Big Ears Animal Sanctuary.

'It loosely began after our trip to Egypt in December 2003 and January 2004. We had some land and we were building a house on that land. And we came home from Egypt and were on the lookout for animals in need of help, so, of course, you open your eyes to them and they're everywhere. We started taking the animals in and it progressed really quickly. We had no idea that there were so many animals in need, especially farm animals. It was quite an eye-opener. We kept growing and growing and we realised that if we were going to ask the community for support in terms of donations we would need to legitimise ourselves, so then we became incorporated. We then applied for charity status and it all came together in 2009.'

Jacqui and Brett had been supporting their work out of their own pockets until that time. Even now, they still sometimes need to take their own money to pay the gaps left by fundraising.

'When we set it up, we were supporting it ourselves. That's our commitment to the animals. We'll do it and if we have to pay for it we will. It's only money. At the end of the day, when you see the difference you can make I would rather have a pen full of bunnies running around happily than money in the bank or new clothes.'

Their twenty-five acres is filled with cows, sheep, donkeys, ponies, goats, pigs, chickens, roosters, turkeys, rabbits, guinea pigs and dozens of cats. The cats live in comfortable outdoor enclosures, most of which Brett built himself. He says he didn't even know how to hold a hammer before that.

'You just do what you have to do,' he says pragmatically.

'One group of ten cats lived on the northern beaches and the lady who was looking after them rang me up,' Jacqui says. 'She was dying and it was her dying wish to capture them all and for them to come and live here and they would never have to live on the beach again. So we agreed. She brought them in over the period of a year. She got them all. We desexed and vaccinated them. They're not friendly, there's no way we're ever going to be able to pick them up. But they're coming around.'

Inside the hospital, which is a shed near the house, animals fill rows of cages and pens on the floor. Some are injured, some have just arrived and are going through quarantine or transition. Some are sick. Several volunteers help clean cages, feed them and tend to wounds, following instructions written on paper and pegged to the doors. Caring for that many animals brings an intense workload. It takes all day and into the night to care for them. Jacqui says her dad is the biggest voluntary support and is there every day. Retirees, veterinary nurses, and people with disabilities or mental health conditions make up the other volunteers. They come via word of mouth and now make Jacqui's day easier than it was before.

Jacqui and Brett live in a tiny 1940s house on top of a hill.

'We originally lived next door on the acreage there but then we wondered why we had this massive house when we were never inside and we could do so much more for the animals. We sold that property and bought this land, which is beautiful and flat, and we put a cheap house on it. We wanted to put all our money into the animals and we don't need much, as long as we've got shelter.'

Egypt has had a profound affect on Jacqui, directly influencing her life path not just once, but twice.

'We went to Egypt in our early twenties and on that trip, I saw a man crawling through his own urine and no one helping him, and I thought I would like to help him. So that gave me the idea of going back to uni to study social work.'

The rest of that holiday went really well and Jacqui and Brett loved it so much they decided to go back one day.

'So we went back for a holiday ten years later. And I don't know if it was a different time, or we were different, but when we went back the second time it just shocked us. We were vegetarians by then and the animal welfare issues were right in our faces. We got in the car to go from the airport to the hotel and we were seeing animals in the traffic in awful conditions, and everywhere we went from then on, we had tears constantly. It was horrible.'

On the first day, Jacqui and Brett witnessed scenes of cruelty, neglect and ignorance over and over again.

'There was a man leading a donkey through traffic and the donkey was hauling a huge trailer stacked high with parcels. The donkey fell down in the traffic from the weight of it and the man beat him relentlessly until he staggered back to his feet. Further on, a man was trying to lure a dog into the traffic so it would be hit.

'After that we just couldn't shut our eyes. It was everywhere. Even where we were staying at the hotel they said to us, "If you love animals, don't go to the Cairo Zoo because you will be sad." Everywhere we went we saw more and more. We'd be sitting down, having a meal, and there would be all these stray, mangy cats that just looked terrible, meowing beside us begging for food, and the wait staff would come out and kick them. At night in bed we could hear the horses clip-clopping along, working twenty-four hours a day taking tourists around. They never stopped. It was endless. It would keep us awake at night because we could hear these poor horses and we knew they never got a rest.'

They were so moved by the animals they encountered, they did some investigations and found the Brooke Hospital for Animals, an international organisation that works to improve the lives of working horses, donkeys and mules in very poor countries. They decided to go there and see if they could help in some way.

'The bad part about it, I guess, is that they're only patching them up to get them back out to work again. We donated a lot of our spending money on the animals there. We saw horses with big holes in their back where their harnesses had worn away their flesh down to the bone.'

There is a photo of Brett kneeling next to one such horse in the stall at the hospital, his face thick with emotion.

'At the time I was in a state of shock,' he says. 'As a police officer, I had attended to many human injuries as a result of car accidents, workplace accidents and assaults, but injuries to animals of this nature were completely foreign to me. I wasn't feeling any anger at that stage, just complete empathy for the animals. The animals just looked so sad. Most of the wounds the horses and donkeys had were as a result of neglect.'

'We went to the pyramids and all we could focus on was the donkey over in the corner being fed cardboard,' Jacqui says. 'It was no longer about wonderful images like the pyramids. Instead, we were seeing other images that we couldn't get away from.

'But we went from being sad in our first week to mad in the second week. We saw these kids in the street who were beating their donkey with big sticks and we just yelled at them to stop. We couldn't keep quiet after that. We started telling people to feed their horses and stop being so cruel.

'After two and a half weeks of torture for us in Egypt, where we'd relentlessly discussed what we could do, I said to Brett that when we got home I really wanted to drop down to part-time work and build a place on our land where we could take in animals, particularly donkeys. I didn't know if there was a need in Tasmania for help for donkeys because we hadn't focused on that before. So we got home and I opened my eyes to what was around me and who needed help and we came across our first donkeys, which weren't actually in need as such. They weren't abused or mistreated but they were going to be bred and we thought, well, if we could stop that we would.

'We got to know the breeder and she came to see our way of thinking and decided she was getting out of it and wouldn't breed them any more. She had lots of offers for her stock but she wanted us to have them and she had her jack gelded at the age of twenty-five so he could live with us. From there we took in our first steer, then goats, and it just continued.

'Donkeys have wonderful personalities and are very gentle and caring. They can also be playful and they have the most beautiful big ears and deep soulful eyes. I love everything about donkeys, even their tendency to be a little stubborn at times, and their braying brings a smile to my face.

'We have had "special" donkeys, especially two that have passed away. Pedro and Kelly were both rescue donkeys and in their mid thirties when they came to live with us. They were so gentle and sweet, and Pedro, who had been mistreated, learned to love and trust again while in our care. I think that this made him very special to a lot of people, including our barefoot hoof trimmer, who spent a lot of time with Pedro. Pedro's inclusion into the donkey herd was amazing; he came alive among his friends and loved them dearly. He stood valiantly beside Kelly when she had to be put to sleep. They were very special, as are the rest of the herd and our other donkey, Bubby, who also passed away.

'The ponies we have seem to come from a background of people getting them as pets either for themselves or for their children. Then they lose interest in the animals and they don't maintain the upkeep with their hooves and general training. Eventually the ponies become "problem" ponies, which really just means they have been ignored and neglected.'

Jacqui and Brett are living their truth – walking the walk, and putting their money where their mouths are. Jacqui stepped back from paid social work positions and Brett volunteered his time as president of the Tasmanian board of the RSPCA, and directed his role as a police prosecutor towards prosecuting animal cruelty cases.

'He worked really hard on those cases, taking them to court and making passionate submissions, and he managed to get the first period of imprisonment in Tasmania for animal cruelty for a man who starved his dog to death.'

As a social worker by trade, Jacqui was already geared towards compassion and service to others. And, with an endless supply of animals in need and a huge and generous heart, setting limits on the intake is a constant challenge.

'It's really hard. Brett tries to help set limits but what I do now is to take any enquiry for new intakes to the board, so it's not just left up to me and my very soft heart. It gives me a cooling-off period to sit back and look at whether or not we can take another animal on when we have so many, to decide whether or not we can do it justice.'

The board is a bunch of highly educated people, comprised of three social workers (including Jacqui), a police officer (Brett) and a professor of ethics.

Jacqui says that as a child she was always very sensitive towards animals and animal cruelty and would become very upset over news items she saw.

'I can still recall those news items, they had that much impact. I was already wired that way, very empathetic towards animals. I was never allowed to have a lot of pets, but I had birds and they were my best friends, they were my everything. It didn't take much to push me towards being a vegetarian in my twenties. One of my friends and colleagues came in one day and said, "I know how much you love animals, so why are you eating them?" I couldn't respond. She was right. Why was I doing that? So I just stopped then and there and became vegetarian and Brett soon followed suit.'

Then in 2006, both Jacqui and Brett read Peter Singer's book, *Animal Liberation*, and that was a catalyst for another life change.

'We realised that it wasn't enough to be vegetarian, in fact it's nowhere near enough, and we became vegan.

'My original plan when I left work and we set ourselves up here was to build an education barn and start having school groups and other groups come through. In 2008 we went to upstate New York and went to Farm Sanctuary, which is the biggest and first of its kind in the world, and we just love how they do things there and how it worked. They were getting the message across to people in a really great way. Not only do you get the educational component, but you then get to go and meet the animals. We wanted to do something like that, but we just don't have the financial backing. And then along came my second diagnosis in 2011 of terminal cancer. So it kind of put the brakes on in terms of what we could do.'

Even so, Big Ears has grown far beyond their original vision.

'I never imagined it becoming as big as it has and I now believe it will get far bigger,' Brett says. 'It has outgrown Jacqui and me and simply wouldn't exist today without the donor support and volunteers.'

Jacqui had originally been diagnosed with a stage-one breast cancer in 2006.

'It felt significant at the time, but I just needed a lumpectomy and radiation and I was right to go. I had check-ups after that and I was fine. So we were just doing our own thing here and working away with the animals and I got really sick, started vomiting and breaking bones. I was here on my own, working flat out all day while Brett was working full-time, as I didn't have volunteers then. And then one day I was just so sick I went into the doctor and it was stage-four breast cancer.

'It was all through my bones, all through my body, so it was straight into chemo. I became very sick and had to be hospitalised and had ten blood transfusions that went neutropenic, which means the neutrophils in my blood were just not able to produce any white blood cells. I was basically on death's door, just steps away from the big chicken coop in the sky. Somehow through all that, I fought back and got through it, did six months of chemo and that ended in December of 2011.

'Then in April 2012 we went to the United States again. And

I don't know why I thought I'd be able to go there; I was so sick the whole time. But it had been something I'd been looking forward to and it was great. We came back and now I've just been living with the knowledge that I probably don't have a lot of time left. I'm on top of it at the moment, which is the good news. And I keep myself very focused on the animals.

'Two weeks after we came back from the United States we were buying out the rabbit meat farm in Hobart and bringing three hundred rabbits home. I just put myself into doing stuff and the animals come first. If I'm sick, too bad. I've got to get out there and do it for them and I think it's that passion and drive that's kept me going. And with that came the realisation that this has got to continue even after I'm gone and even after Brett's gone, that's why we've got it set up this way. We don't have children and so there's no one else for us to leave anything to. It will continue as it is now for the animals. That's our goal for it.

'I'll stay here for as long as I can. If we have to get a nurse in, we'll do that. I'm not leaving this place. I try to be very mindful not to take on too many animals because it's not about what I can look after any more, it's about what everyone else can look after when I'm gone. That's why having such a great bunch of volunteers is so important. I want them to realise that this is their place as much as ours and have a sense of ownership over what we're doing because one day we will totally rely on them to run it.'

While the Egyptian horses and donkeys were the catalyst for this huge life change, Jacqui wants to make it clear she's not targeting Egypt as exceptional in its treatment of animals.

'It just happened to be the right time and I just happened to be in the right mental space to see what was going on, as opposed to being a tourist who just cruises around and somehow doesn't see it. And that's pretty much how people live their lives every day. They just cruise along and point the finger. For example, we point our fingers at Egypt for the animal cruelty in their abattoirs and people get really passionate about it and all I can think is, *What do you think goes on here?* Really, do you think there isn't an element of cruelty that goes on when a lot of ex-criminals – violent criminals – work in these places?

'I was in a unique position because I worked with young offenders and a lot of them would go on to pick up positions in the local meatworks. So I know from what they would tell me, and from what those people are actually like themselves, what's going on. And these people are violent young men – they hurt people, they hurt animals, and then they get a job on the kill floor, which legitimises and legalises their favourite sport, which is hurting anyone, be it an animal or a person. I recall one person, an incredibly violent young man who was working in there, actually said to me, "I can't stomach it any more, it's gross what goes on on the kill floors." That's always stayed with me. If he's grossed out by it, then there's something really wrong.

'I think it's easy for other people to point fingers at other countries, and rightly so because what's going on is horrendous, but it's that comfort zone that they don't have to look at themselves and what they're participating in by buying products that are coming from meatworks. Do they really think that it's all lovely out there and that these animals are humanely treated and slaughtered in a comfortable and pain-free fashion? Of course not. It's scary, it's bloody, it's dirty, it's gross. And often the people working there are low on empathy themselves because they're already lacking in that area through their own issues and backgrounds of abuse and violence.'

There was nothing substantial that Jacqui or Brett could do for the Egyptian donkeys and horses as tourists in a country on the other side of the world for just a couple of weeks. They spent as much time as they could at the Brooke Hospital, and their time there with the injured and starving horses and donkeys did its work of showing them what they could do back home. And that was to look at their life and their own country and start in their own backyard.

'I remember sitting in a hotel room and saying to Brett that this was really what I wanted to do. I had been quite ambitious with my work as a social worker, I wanted to get further in what I was doing, but then that just didn't seem to matter any more. I really wanted to do whatever I could with the animals, knowing that it's going on all around us in Australia – we just hide it better. Once your eyes are opened you can't close them again.'

'I see the same welfare issues for equines as I do for all other animals. The lack of animal welfare and animal rights means that many animals suffer in our society. People see animals as 'property' and as such tend to forget that these animals have their own needs and wants and rights. People tend to view animals as dispensable, and will get a pony or horse and then when they lose interest they either neglect the animal or they move the animal on to someone else.'

For Brett, he sees the horse racing industry as one of the biggest threats to horse welfare in this country.

'There's a need to breed thousands of horses every year so that the odd one or two can make money for people, but the reality is that most end up in slaughter yards.'

It is a gloriously mild late spring day, with blue skies and a warm sun, and Jacqui invites me into their small home for a cup of coffee. As I settle into the couch, a large, pure-white rabbit with red eyes and a twitching nose hops around the corner, climbs up onto the couch, sits next to me and begins to chew my buttons.

'This is Wiseman,' Jacqui says. 'He's already been featured in a book.'

As a Queenslander, and therefore not lawfully permitted to keep a rabbit of my own, there's a special kind of magic in sharing my coffee with Wiseman. It's like he's a vision or a character from a movie.

Wiseman was one of the rabbits who came from the meat farm, taken from a cramped cage in a dark shed, living under similar conditions to battery hens, likely having never even walked on grass. Wiseman decided of his own accord that he should live inside the house, rather than out in the bunny pens, and is often the 'spokesman' for the charity.

'I remember when I hit that wall of grief after being diagnosed, I was thinking, *I don't want to leave the animals*, and I would sit and cry and cry. *I want to see Wiseman grow older*. I wasn't ready to give up. That was a huge part of it. I would get Brett to bring pictures to me in hospital and I'd want a run-down on everything that was going on while I was having blood pumped into me to try and save my life. I never focused on the treatment. I was always focused on what was going on with this and what was going on with that. I never allowed myself a moment to worry about me. When I did come home and I was bedridden for a lot of the time, I'd get Brett to take me out to see the animals and I'd walk as far as I could and see as many as I could in that short amount of time before I had to go back to bed, and that just lifted me for the day. I'd get back in bed, vomiting my heart out, but I'd be thinking, *Oh, I saw Buster and he was running around.*

'It's just second nature for me to put the animals first, so that's what I did. I put the animals first right throughout my illness. I even recall having a huge argument with my oncologist one day about going home to the farm, to the animals. I was in lockdown, in an area where no one was allowed without masks because any little illness would have killed me, and he said to me, "I can guarantee if you go home and a chook so much as sneezes on you, you'll be coming back in a body bag tonight." And that just shows where my focus was. I wasn't thinking about me, that I was so sick that I could die that easily, I was just thinking I wanted to see the animals. One of our rescue dogs, Lucas, just lives for me. His whole focus is me. So I would worry the whole time about how he was coping.'

The amount of pain medication Jacqui is on makes her very tired. She needs to have a big sleep every afternoon, after most of the day's work is done. Then when Brett comes home they do more work together and then she's back in bed around six-thirty in the evening.

'I know that in reality I've probably got two years, if I'm lucky.

But I don't plan on sticking to that schedule. I just take it as it comes. I guess I'm quite at peace with the inevitability but I'm not giving up just yet. I just enjoy every day that I'm here with the animals. Every day that I'm able to see them and pat them, I'm really blessed. I think part of being at peace with it is knowing that it doesn't stop with me. It's bigger than me and it's going to continue without me. And that's great. That's a wonderful thing. It's really comforting to know that I can pass away and these animals aren't just going to be left in the lurch. Hopefully this will continue for sixty years from now.'

When it comes to animal welfare, Brett says that people need to change their focus.

'It's not all about saving apes, whales and tigers. The best thing anyone can do for animals is to go vegan. Help spare some of the millions of animals that are killed every day for our food. A chicken in a battery cage or a sow in a sow stall has the same feelings as a "celebrity" animal such as a whale. I'm not saying that saving celebrity animals isn't a great cause but you can do so much just by changing your lifestyle choices.

'It can be really tough dealing with the frustration. Change seems to take forever. In my experience, people are really ignorant of animal welfare issues on the big scale and prefer to stay that way. I am often told, "Don't tell me that or I will never eat meat again," rather than, "I wasn't aware of that but now I know I might think about what I choose to eat."'

Jacqui is already leaving an incredible legacy in the world and has been a source of inspiration for people everywhere. I ask her what messages she's hoping people will take away from her story.

'I would like people to consider the question that was put to me: if you love animals, why are you eating them? I think that we're species-ist in this country, and in a lot of countries, and there is a certain amount of empathy and outrage around certain animals, and there are other animals, like horses and rabbits and birds, that just miss out on our caring. There is no difference between what happens to cows or sheep in abattoirs than there is to what happens to horses. We just need to extend our empathy towards all animals.

'The other thing is that I often get messages from people who say that if they won the lotto they'd do what we're doing, and I feel like saying, "Well, just do it! Just go and do it!" I did it and we didn't have a lot of money to do it. You find a way to work through and do it. If it's important enough to you, you'll find a way.'

BOO

Standing in a paddock in Point Cook in Melbourne is the most gorgeous pony. Boo is a deep chestnut with white splashes of pinto markings on his shoulders and rump and a lighter, gingery mane. Investigations into his past reveal 'good breeding' in his genes, with a champion show-ring sire and breeders who were passionate about the Australian Riding Pony breed, and pintos in particular. He is elegant, with huge, expressive eyes, and is the love of the Gilbee family, and sixteen-year-old Jennah Gilbee in particular. But life could have turned out very differently for this pony.

Boo might have been bred with wonderful intentions, but he ended up in the hands of someone who didn't have the knowledge or respect to work with him. He was beaten and terrorised, and when a council worker approached the owner one day as the horse was being whipped, the owner simply handed the pony over in disgust. The council worker then passed Boo over to Project Hope Horse Welfare Victoria for rehabilitation. And, just as it takes a village to raise a child, it took a whole herd of people to achieve that rehabilitation.

When Boo first arrived into the charity's care, his extreme fear and flight response initiated an instant decision from his carers that he would only ever be able to be rehomed as a companion horse. The first carer had him for some time but didn't have the time to do much with him.

Then Jennifer Burchat came onto the scene.

'There are a lot of strange things that have surrounded Boo's story. I wasn't a member of Project Hope. I rang Project Hope once, enquiring about how you go about getting a lease horse from them, and I don't even know if I left my details. Then about twelve months later, I had a phone call from the president, Sue Kirkguard. I don't know why. I wasn't a member. She asked me if I would be able to take Boo on short-term care, but in his case she expected it to actually be long-term because of the problems that he had. He wasn't just skinny and neglected; he was abused and scared.'

Jennifer had recently temporarily taken on a horse that needed a new home. She told Sue that if she found a home for Humphrey in the next couple of weeks then she would be able to take the pony.

'And lo and behold, two days later, my trimmer was here trimming the horses and said, if I ever wanted to find a home for Humphrey, he knew a perfect couple that would absolutely love him. And I said, "Oh, really? Isn't that odd!" It was a perfect home for him and only about twenty minutes up the road. So I thought, *Gosh, now I'll have to ring Sue back and tell her I'll take that pony!*

'Boo arrived and he was an absolutely beautiful little pony. But terrified of people. He was like a little child in a schoolyard that looks as though everyone is going to pick on him. All the other horses did pick on him, even the ones that didn't normally pick on horses. He had it written all over him. Luckily, I work from home so I had the time for him that he needed.

'When he came to me, the first thing I wanted to do was to be able to catch him reliably. I didn't really believe I had the tools I needed for this little fella; he had a lot of problems. I thought I'd just try to gain his trust. So to get him to be caught reliably, I used Monty Roberts' Join-Up process and that seemed to work really well with him. Join-Up builds a conversation and you're saying to the horse, "Well, I know where you're coming from, I can speak to you and we can have a conversation here, even though I'm a predator and you're a prey animal."

'I find when you're working with a scared pony and you're trying to get the pony's trust, *you've* got to trust the pony. It's a two-way thing. And that seems to be a really big thing in a horse's mind. So often when we work with horses it's a one-way street; it's about what they can do for us. But when you turn it around a bit and ask what you can do for them, they really understand that. That's something that really resonates in them.

'So I would sit down on the ground a lot while he was eating, sitting at his feet, and make myself vulnerable, and whatever he wanted to do was fine. If he wanted to come over and nibble my hair that was fine, or if he just wanted to stand with me, or if he wanted to go away that was fine too. It was just a matter of hanging out with him, to say somebody really did want to be his friend and be there for him and not pick on him.'

But although Jennifer had come a long way with Boo and gained his trust through her horsemanship, enough to reliably catch him and hang out with him, he still had huge problems with fear of people's movements. Jennifer was open to all advice and willing to try different approaches to move through the pony's fear.

Once again, timing was on Boo's side. Dr Katherine Macmillan, a veterinary behaviourist from Melbourne, offered her services to Project Hope, so Jennifer contacted her to see if she could help Boo.

'She asked me which main behavioural problem was stopping Boo from being rehabilitated. I said it was his fear of humans making fast movements. If you went to scratch your face or brush a fly away he'd be in the next county before you could blink. He was very quick. So she set up a program for me and it was not to desensitise him but to actually change the neural pathways so that when he sees a fast movement, instead of thinking he's going to be hit he thinks he's going to get a treat. No matter how the horse reacts, you give him his favourite treat. I did that for about ten minutes twice a day for ten days and that was the end of the problem.'

This approach is not a traditional one in the school of horsemanship.

'I'm open to everything. It's not really about horsemanship; it's about the way the brain works. Instead of that behaviour (me jumping or throwing my arms around) meaning something bad, that behaviour now means something good. And you don't have to continue with the treats after the behaviour has changed. Once it's changed, that's it and it won't go back to the old way unless you start hitting him again.'

Dr Macmillan remembers Boo well.

'It is common for horses to react fearfully to rapid movements. As prey animals they tend to do so quite naturally, but this reaction will be enhanced if they have been physically punished by people and associate sudden movements with pain.

'Fearful reactions often do not involve conscious thought. There are fear circuits present in the brain that "bypass" the rational brain – the cerebral cortex. The idea is to build a new association to the "stimulus". If every time Boo sees a sudden movement, something good happens to him, the movement will start to predict the good experience and Boo will react less fearfully. Through repetition, the horse may start to see the movement as a good thing and look forward to the treat that follows. We describe this process as "counter-conditioning".

'Imagine you are incredibly fearful of snakes. Possibly seeing a snake makes you scream, break into a sweat or, probably, run in the opposite direction. Imagine if a snake appeared in the room you were currently in. How would you react? Now imagine if every time you saw a snake, I was to give you ten thousand dollars in cash. Would your attitude to snakes change? You may even begin searching for them to earn your reward!

'But there are a few conditions that need to be met if counter-conditioning is to be successful. In the example with the snakes, it wouldn't work if you were actually bitten by a snake! This might actually make you more fearful of snakes in the end, the opposite of what is intended.

'In terms of Boo, this means that Jennifer couldn't be *too* scary. For this reason we combine counter-conditioning with desensitisation. Jennifer needed to start with small movements or stand further away from Boo during the process and progressively make movements more scary.

'It's also necessary to provide sufficient reward. With the snake example, if I had offered one dollar for every snake sighting, most people would still run away. The same applies to horses – you have to provide sufficient reward to make it a positive experience and for the learning to occur. Recent research has shown that food is a far more effective reward than pats or praise for horses, so I recommend owners find a tasty morsel and use this to make their training as powerful and effective as possible.'

To further Boo's chances of finding a great home, Project Hope decided to send him for training, to be started under saddle. But given Boo is only 12 hands high, the trainer couldn't do much riding with him because he was too big for him. So Jennifer continued his education when he returned to her house.

'I rode him a bit when he came back. He dumped me twice. He was still very afraid of doing the wrong thing and not knowing what the wrong thing was. So he was very afraid of doing anything and getting it wrong and bearing the consequences.'

Jennifer had been a keen student of many different forms of natural horsemanship communication and training methods. 'I've probably been to ten or twelve different clinicians over the time that I've had horses. I just love learning. But it was Boo who led me to Parelli. And I really feel Parelli's the way to go. Parelli is all based on the horse. It's not about what you want and what you want to do with the horse. It's about the horse and your relationship with the horse. And I really like that. That really rings true to me that that's the way it should be.

'When it came to Boo, I just felt I didn't have enough tools to help him. It wasn't just a matter of getting him used to things. He was perfectly fine around cars and dogs and domestic things like that. *People* were his problem. So I took him to a couple of clinics and started to learn Parelli and I found that really helped and it gave me something to do with him and a way of having a conversation to show that although I was a predator, I wasn't going to eat him.

'He particularly liked just getting out on the streets and walking around and looking at things. I kept going with him because he really, really wanted to connect. He really wanted to befriend somebody. He had this real desire to get better. He was so brave. And those kinds of horses are really worth putting in the effort for.'

Jennifer's progress with Boo brings her a lot of satisfaction, both in terms of her own achievement with him and in terms of what he can show other people.

'A lot of people who would have given up on him at the start see him now having a normal life and being ridden and loved, and they realise you don't just give up on a horse because he's not doing what you want him to do. They can see that you really can turn a horse around. There aren't good horses and bad horses; there are just horses.'

Boo's size actually added complexity to his rehabilitation. He was too small for an adult and too flighty for a child.

'So Jennah was the perfect partner for him,' Jennifer says.

Jennah Gilbee was fourteen when she became Boo's person.

'When we got him he wasn't really broken-in properly. He

was scared of pretty much everyone and everything. So we had to do a lot of work with him but he's a lot better now and runs up to you in the paddock and plays games with you.'

Jennah had always wanted a horse. Her father, Mark Gilbee, says, 'We started taking her to lessons when she was about five, hoping that would satisfy her, but it didn't. We used to call her a nature's child. She loved anything to do with animals or that involved being outside in the garden.'

Jennah has two brothers but no one else in the family was really interested in horses.

'The boys have been pretty good with Boo. They've both got their licences now and both of them have had to take Jennah down a couple of times to help feed him. They like to be down there and pat him. But they don't do anything else,' Mark says.

Boo is agisted five minutes from the Gilbees' house. They go down straight after school or whenever Therese (Jennah's mother) or Mark is home to go with her. 'We get to scoop the poop while she gets to have fun with the horse,' Mark says good-naturedly.

'Initially, there was a horse that came up for sale at one of the riding schools Jennah goes to and it was one of her favourites, so she was on our back and looking at a multitude of websites of horse sales and trying to do deals with us. That was how she got onto Project Hope's website and saw an advertisement for Boo under a free lease. We made an initial enquiry via phone and heard nothing from them. We put a request in online to say we were interested in the horse, but still didn't hear anything.'

But again, fortunes were on Boo's side. Joy, a family friend of the Gilbees, has a cabin up in the high country and welcomes the Gilbees on occasion to stay with her and ride her horses. One night Joy emailed with information about a horse she thought Jennah might be interested in.

'And it was the exact same horse we'd enquired about with Project Hope!' Mark says. 'So I rang Joy and she said that a lady she worked with, Jennifer Burchat, was caring for Boo and Joy had seen Jennifer's flyer and thought of Jennah. So I think it was pretty much meant to be.

'We got back onto Project Hope and decided to go up and meet Boo at the foster home, which was about a two-hour drive. We spent most of the day up there and Jennah lunged him a little bit but he was really, really scared of people. We had to stand right back from where he was working and go nowhere near him because he was very flighty, obviously because he'd been mistreated. Following that, Jennah went back up for a horse clinic and watched how they did all the natural horsemanship and they assessed Jennah while she was riding Boo. It was a bit of a test to see if she could handle him and it all went pretty well.

'About a month later, he was delivered to a property here in Melbourne where they could keep an eye on Boo and keep an eye on Jennah. He was down at that property for about three months. The property owner there breaks in horses and said Jennah was more than capable. She said Jennah was one of the most accomplished riders she'd met and she listens to everything you tell her and had no problem recommending that we take Boo away as soon as we had a property ready.'

Jennah hadn't been specifically looking for a rescue horse when she began her search. 'When I first saw his picture I thought he was a cute horse. I read his description and from the things they said he seemed to have had it pretty rough. But it also said that he was quick to learn and always wanted to please, so I figured he'd make a good pony and a good friend.'

Jennah wasn't put off by the fact that Boo had some issues that needed to be worked through. 'Most of the horses I used to ride at the riding school had issues, so I was pretty used to it by then. I just tried to see what he was afraid of and then tried to get him used to those things. To start off with, he was afraid of men. So I'd get Dad to come and stand near him and pat him and give him food and treats. He was also afraid of pushbikes, so we got an old bicycle and stood it up in his paddock. We fed him near it until he got used to it and wasn't afraid of it any more.'

'And now he just pushes the bike over,' Mark says. 'Every time we go down there the bike's lying down again. Once when we were with Jennah while she was riding him down to the beach and we could see some kids on bikes coming. We said to Jennah to get off him and hold him, and he seemed to go okay with it. So the next step is, when the weather's a bit better, I'm going to take my bike down into the paddock and see what he does. Eventually we hope that Therese and I could ride our bikes beside him while Jennah's riding down to the beach.'

For a family that was largely uninvolved in horses, Boo has become a bit of a shared project.

'It's been interesting,' Mark says. 'It's a big difference from when Jennah was going to a horseriding school and having fun all day and us not knowing what was going on or having to worry too much about it, to all of a sudden having a horse we have to feed every night. We've got to tend to his hooves, and make sure he's wormed, and do this and do that.' He pauses. 'And scoop the poop, of course.'

They've also had to deal with Boo injuring himself, smashing his knee on the side of a horse float and cutting it open so it needed five stitches, bandaging and medicine. 'I've got notes from the vet because I've been keeping a file on Boo. Every time we worm him or get his hooves trimmed or any kind of major event I keep a note on it.'

It's clear the family is committed to Boo.

'We love him – probably pretty much to death,' Mark laughs.

To bring Boo into the family, the Gilbees had to jump through a lot of organisational hoops and tick a lot of boxes. They were watched over for months in the early stage of Boo's arrival. If they'd gone and bought any horse out of the newspaper they wouldn't have had to do any of that. Was it a valuable experience?

'Yes, it was,' Mark says. 'Boo was a mistreated horse so I suppose that made it a bit more difficult. We could have bought a horse out of the paper but we wouldn't have had that extra support. Certainly, having those people there to support us and give us tips has been useful. Although, what we have learned is that everyone has their own opinion about things and everyone does things differently and they're forthright about expressing it, so that can be frustrating too.

'But we can't thank those people enough for the effort they've gone to in order to work with Boo and get him ready for us. It's all flowed pretty easily. We put a lot of trust in Jennah and she's proven she does know a fair bit about horses. The steepest learning curves have probably been dealing with his injury and the vet, and working with him to get Boo confident getting on and off the horse float.

'It's been a big thing in Jennah's life, something she's always wanted. And that comes with responsibility too. But she's been really good with her responsibility. She's really good on the anatomy of the horse. Every time we're there she brushes him and cleans his hooves, and checks him all over to make sure he's okay. She taught me recently how to put the halter on. When I got it on last week to put him in the float, I think it worked – it looked right. Buying the float was another thing we had to worry about; that was a fair bit of research into what we wanted and what car we needed, what towing capacity and so on.'

Jennah, though, seems to have taken it all in her stride. 'The troubled horses I used to ride at the riding school got me used to the kind of things that Boo did too, being afraid of everything and needing some help along the way.'

Jennah has taken Boo to a smattering of pony club events but says that, although he did very well, it's not really her biggest passion though she enjoys the games.

'Project Hope has a policy that says if you've had a horse for five years you can apply for ownership. So I plan on doing that after five years. I plan on keeping him for a while.'

'I think forever,' Mark clarifies. 'Even if she outgrows him he'll stay as much a part of the family because we just love him.'

That feeling of love has been transformative for Jennah. 'When we got him, I'd always been desperate for a horse and my parents kept saying no. Then when they said I could lease a horse I jumped at the chance when I found Boo. And once we had him he just brightened everything up. I do school work better now.'

Mark agrees. 'She *does* do school work better now. She used to be a little bit slack in doing homework.'

'Doing everything,' Jennah says.

'Yeah, doing everything. And it's not that we've made any threats about not being able to spend time with Boo if she doesn't do her homework, I think it's just helped her out with life. She's more engaged with school. When she has to write a short story, she writes about Boo. And we've seen her marks get better. She's got someone in her life that she takes care of and nurtures and that's been a big excitement. That's just carried on into her schoolwork.'

'I had a persuasive speech to do where I had to get people on my side about something and I did mine on shutting down knackeries,' Jennah says.

Mark explains. 'There's one down here near us and she researched it and there's some pretty shocking video footage on the web and she wrote a whole essay on it and did her presentation, but they wouldn't let her play the film clips because they thought it might be upsetting for some students.'

'I included Boo in that because with his abusive history he could have easily ended up in a knackery. So I talked about how his life changed when I got him. And the point is that can happen for all kinds of horses, wherever they're rescued from. That speech got good marks. It got a ninety.'

Jennah's speech is confronting, even for someone like me who was immersed in that sort of information for the three years I ran the horse rescue charity. She details flawed slaughtering attempts; callous treatment of horses through the abattoir; the plights of pregnant mares, foals and small horses through the transport and yard system; the horror of the ill-management of injured horses; and the gruesome realities of the fates of so many racehorses. It's painful, difficult stuff.

She is clearly passionate about animals and welfare issues and has begun to look to where her future might lie in that field.

'She said she wanted to be an RSPCA inspector or something like that,' Mark says. 'Then an opportunity for work experience with the mounted police came up and she had to write an essay to be selected. We had no input into that and when I read it I was very impressed. It was very from the heart, and a lot of research went into it. Then the school congratulated her and she was the only one who got selected for the mounted police force. And she had to do another letter to the mounted branch itself.'

'It was quite interesting,' Jennah says. 'When I went to the mounted branch, I got to help train one of the newer horses they were getting into the squad. That was fun. And I got to muck up lots of poo. I was always interested in the police force, but it was after I got Boo that I got interested in the mounted police force.'

For having suffered an awful start with humans, Boo's come a very long way. Once terrified, he's now affectionate, following Jennah around, nuzzling her and looking to her for treats.

'His favourites right now are liquorice and pears. Once when we were having a picnic, I got off him and went to have a drink and when I came back he'd walked right into the middle of eight or nine people and was eating someone's sandwich.'

Mark says, 'He's a people horse now. He can still be a bit flighty but he calms down quickly. Jennah hugs him and kisses him. He's comfortable with her now.'

It's easy to see how much the Gilbees adore Boo.

Jennah's mother, Therese, says, 'Boo's a very cute little horse.

He's someone else in our life to love. The main thing has been the joy to see the change in him. When I think of that first day when we saw him, he just kept glancing across to Mark and me with this look of fear. But then just last Sunday, when I was scooping the poop, Jennah was following me around, sitting on Boo, and Boo was following me around, and every time I stopped to pick up the poo I couldn't even turn around again because he was right there behind me. He wouldn't do that before.'

Jennah says she is simply happier since Boo's been in her life.

'She's certainly not one of those ratbag teenagers,' Mark says. 'For someone who's sixteen she's pretty much just into sport, her horse and being outdoors, and with any sort of animals. Jennah will often sleep in till midday or later, but on the days when it might be pony club or we have to do something special with Boo, she's up at seven o'clock as quick as a shot. But any other time, she's hard to wake up and hard to get motivated in the morning.'

And Mark adds, 'She's pretty proud, too. She's quite keen for all her friends to know she has a horse.'

'And they're quite happy to say they want to steal him,' she says.

There is one more who has benefited from Boo's journey – this time, a fellow horse.

Boo's foster carer, Jennifer Burchat, says, 'I had a bit of a problem horse: Safire. She's a Morgan–Arab cross. She could be very challenging. I did a lot of courses trying to get inside her head. Initially, I looked at all the possible physical reasons – saddle fit and so on – and after a while I realised maybe it wasn't that at all, but the relationship and the way I was handling her. I actually sold that horse.

'Two years later, I bought her back because after I had Boo and got into Parelli, I understood her better and I knew where I went wrong with her. So I bought her back because the people who took her couldn't handle her and she was on a downward spiral. Now I'm working with her with Parelli and she's great. There was nothing wrong with the horse – it was *me*. I wouldn't have bought Safire back if it hadn't been for Boo. That's how much he changed me.'

And Jennah couldn't be happier that there is one more 'problem horse' that won't be heading to a knackery, all because of Boo and the people whose lives have changed just from knowing him.

LARRY

Exiting the dense and stressful traffic of the highways and roads around the Gold Coast, I finally find myself driving through sleepy streets in a pocket of green, bordered by post-and-rail fences and dotted with grazing horses and cows. Sue Spence says her place is idyllic, and she's not wrong. It's the place she came to, along with her family, after she'd been diagnosed with breast cancer.

Inside her one-and-a-half-acre hideaway, she now runs horsemanship lessons in a purpose-built, raised and levelled arena under a shady tree, with a wooden grandstand from where parents and carers can watch. On the day I visit, there are two young girls there for a session and another four who are helpers, mostly former students now doing work experience with Sue to continue their development. The girls here today have been referred by their psychiatrist and psychologist.

'Larry has opened hundreds of hearts, and I mean *hundreds*. Children come here, who aren't kids any more, and Larry opens their heart and they become children once again.'

Little Larry is cute and rotund and his sides wobble as he trots on his wee legs. He's a white miniature pony and is the smallest horse on Sue's property, even smaller than her Shetlands, Mindy and Yogi, and a pixie pony compared to the towering chestnut quarter horse, Sunny. He was also the final addition to Sue's herd, rescued from the knackery, completing her four-horse team.

When I meet him in the paddock, he instantly follows me and leans into me, giving me his trademark cuddle and, just like every other person who works with Larry, my heart melts. Admittedly, where I'm concerned, that's not too difficult, but still, it is almost inconceivable to imagine how this sweet, soft pony ended up in an abattoir.

But when Sue picks up a lead rope to ever so gently ask him to step sideways, his eyes bulge and those little legs hasten to move on to avoid any sort of harsh follow-up. It is then possible to see how, in the wrong hands, Larry might have been misunderstood as a flighty, crazy horse, when in reality he is just super sensitive to anything but the quietest of communication. And it's exactly this that makes him such a special teaching horse, not only for the children and adults who come to work with him, but also for Sue, who was going through an intense healing journey herself right when Larry came along.

Sue's drive to help others was always in her, but it really became the focus of her life after her cancer diagnosis. She was forced to channel that healing inwards for the first time, learn more about herself and what she could teach others, and then go forward and share it.

'It's still traumatic for me. Back then, I was running a really big gym at Robina and I was teaching heaps of classes and I was delivering my fitness programs. It was full on.

'I didn't even have a lump. I went to the doctor for a check-up and just mentioned that my breasts were painful. She said she wanted to send me for an ultrasound, which I couldn't understand because I didn't have a lump. But she just had a feeling.

'I had the ultrasound and I read the report, of course, as you do. It said that there was a calcification and it appeared benign. No worries. I handed it to my doctor and again she just had a feeling and said she wanted a specialist to look at it for another opinion. I went to the specialist and it was cancer. And I didn't even have a lump!

'The treatment plan was to have a lumpectomy, then radiation, then I'd be going onto Tamoxifen – a chemical that alters your hormones. But I told him I'd decided to have a double mastectomy instead. I just wanted them off and I wanted no discussion. I'd made my mind up. It was like having a spider on me and all I wanted to do was get it off.

'I went and had the double mastectomy and it turned out there were early changes in the other breast too. Then I went through nearly another year of reconstruction, which was huge.

'It's affected me tremendously. I ended up with really bad anxiety after all that. Horrendous. It was classed as an anxiety disorder. I was in flight mode all time. That's why I relate to someone who comes to me with anxiety because I know what it looks like. I know what it feels like. It's like an express train roaring through your body when you have bad anxiety. You can't sleep. You can't ever be at peace.'

At the time of diagnosis, Sue and her family were living in a nice home in Burleigh Waters.

'Life was very hectic. I was working in the gym and I was teaching. My youngest was nine and my eldest was seventeen. My mum was living with us as well in a granny flat. And it was go, go, go.

'It had always been my dream to live with my horses. I had always agisted them from such a young age in New Zealand, riding my pushbike to the paddock, wherever it was, with buckets hanging off the handlebars and a saddle balanced on the front and the feed balanced on the back. I would ride a long way into headwinds and sleet. In New Zealand, if you don't go out in that weather then you don't get to see your horse! Talk about being keen! So I grew up like that. Then when I came to Australia and first started getting horses I always agisted, but it's never the same when you're a horse lover. You dream of having a horse at your window.

'I had a horse, Sox, agisted with a friend about a year and a half before my diagnosis but I had to find another home for him, which was really sad, because I couldn't keep him there any more. Life had gotten so busy I just couldn't drive out there every day because of my work commitments.

'Then when I'd had my diagnosis and had gone through the surgery, I just kept driving out here (to Tallebudgera) to get away from town and see a place with horses. It was what I'd always dreamed of. It's so pretty. It had such a lovely vibe about it. The pony club's up the road and it was like the dream area from when I was little. It was time to embrace what I wanted to do. So we said, "Let's just do it."

'I knew I wanted to move. I wanted to start living my life differently. The cancer journey was the reason we moved. When you go through something like that you reassess what you really want in life.' And what she wanted was horses.

She went to buy a miniature stallion, Riley, with the intention of breeding miniature ponies, but came home with two ponies instead.

'I was there to buy Riley but I could hear all these kids yelling and riding around on quad bikes and here was this white Shetland, Mindy, in the midst of all this, with kids being terrifying with quad bikes and sticks. I asked the guy what was going on and he said the kids were just having fun. I said to him it wasn't fun at all – that's not fun for that pony. And I asked him if he'd sell her to me right then because I wanted her too. I just had to take her and get her away from there. She's just the most beautiful, gentle soul. So I bought them both and it turned out she was pregnant with Yogi, which makes it worse because she was being harassed and stressed while pregnant. And Riley was the father.

'Then when little Yogi Bear was born, the vet advised us to put Riley in another paddock just in case he hurt the foal. I put him in with the neighbour's horse and the neighbour's horse kicked him and attacked him and shattered his leg in four places. It was devastating. We would have paid anything for the surgery but the vet advised it may not work and might actually cause pain. I had to euthanase him.'

It was a tremendous blow for Sue at an already emotionally overloaded time. She'd reconnected with horses as a crucial part of her self-healing but now her dream had turned to devastation.

Sue was still looking for a horse for herself to ride when she came across Sunny. She'd always had big Thoroughbreds before this, and Sunny was totally different – smaller, a quarter horse, with a hogged (cut-off) mane. She went to look at him three times before the owner told her that if she wanted to trial him she could take him away for a month and if she decided to keep him she could send him the money. So she did.

'Some time later, I saw Larry's photo online on a rescue site and I thought he looked just like Riley. As soon as I saw Larry's picture, with his little upturned nose, I just knew I had to go and get him. He couldn't go to the abattoir. I had no plan for him other than to save him and I thought I'd rehome him. I've only got a small property and I already had Sunny, Mindy and Yogi. But it didn't turn out that way.

'I found out it's really common for miniature horses to end up at the abattoir. I drove all the way out there but I couldn't even get near him. Larry was really scruffy and it looked as though his feet had never been done. They were all pointy.

'I brought him home but he was so traumatised. He had that lost look in his eyes and it just broke my heart. So I put him in the garden. I couldn't put him in the paddock because he would have been too much of a victim. Yogi would have made minced meat out of him. He was so traumatised that he couldn't stand up for himself. I couldn't get near him. I couldn't pick up a rope or a stick, which made it feel like he'd been hit at some stage. So he lived in the front yard for weeks and I didn't even pressure him, I just left him alone.

'I'd go out with some feed and he'd run to the far end of the yard and stand with his head in the corner and his bum sticking out, trying to hide. So I just put the food down and walked away every day and left it there for him to get when he felt safe. And after doing that for two weeks, I went out one day to feed him and his head was poking out, not his bottom.

'I wanted to yell out, "Good boy!" but I had to make myself stop and say nothing because too much pressure would have frightened him back into his corner. So I just popped the food down and crouched on the ground next to it. I could sense him starting to creep over towards me, so I just breathed out and stayed still and he crept over and stood right over my shoulder. I turned my head and he pushed his little forehead up against mine and I just wanted to cry.'

Just as Sue was taking small steps forward in her own healing, Larry had begun his.

'I wanted to pat him and praise him but I just had to breathe out and gently walk away because if I hadn't walked away at that time he would have lost trust in me because he was so reactive to any sharp movement. Then the next day, I sat there a bit longer.'

Before long, Larry's personality began to surface.

'I kept going out in the morning and finding the outside cushions flung all around the house and I kept going mad on the dog. But then I went out one morning and actually caught the culprit and it wasn't the dog at all – it was Larry! He had one in his mouth and was swinging it and flinging it, cheeky boy. And he looked at me with this glint in his eye as though he was quite proud of himself in that moment.'

Sue says it took years for her to work through her anxiety, but breathing and calming herself was one of the keys to her healing. Her horsemanship practice, which demanded her undivided attention, was also pivotal.

'We used to have Larry-and-me time for quite a few weeks. I sat out there in the garden with him and my book. He'd come over while I was reading and take my book out of my hands and then he'd rest his nose on my tummy while I sat there drinking my cup of tea.'

These weeks gave Sue precious time to find her inner stillness.

'When he was ready, I put him in with the rest of the herd. And now he's the instigator. He'll run around with his tail up in the air like an Arab and revs them all up – but then as soon as they get rough he runs away. Then when they stop playing and calm down he'll start them off again.

'He's such a classic expressive pony. I just love him so much. And it could have ended a lot differently for him.'

Sue has had horses all her life and participated in showjumping and eventing when she was in New Zealand. But it wasn't until she was older and in Australia that she began learning natural horsemanship techniques, which were so much about mastering her own body language and energy.

'I had such an amazing change in myself from starting natural horsemanship and that was why I started to share it. It became a teaching program. Healing my anxiety took a combination of learning how to breathe properly and doing my horsemanship because that's all very focused and calming. The horsemanship helped me work through that trauma immensely. I work a lot with the horses at liberty – with no ropes. Liberty is so good at getting you focused in the moment because if you lose your focus for a second you lose your horse. I began to teach people how to use their body language more effectively and it's just grown out of there. I can't believe it's gone where it has.'

Sue's been running Horses Helping Humans and the charitable Horse Whispering Youth Program full-time for more than seven years. She gets referrals from youth organisations, psychiatrists and the heads of mental health units. As well, her work is well known in universities and she has research students from New South Wales, Brisbane and Ipswich coming to observe her.

Her previous career in the fitness industry has set up a strong foundation for her work today.

'I ran fitness centres for thirty years and I used to run a program educating instructors on how to recognise eating disorders within the fitness industry. A lot of that is how to read body language, how to pick up people's tones, and how to approach people. So that advanced a treat once I began natural horsemanship. Fitness Australia approved that program and for me to travel around and teach it to as many people in the fitness industry as I could, but that's when I was diagnosed with breast cancer. I was just about to start my Australian tour but the breast cancer sent me in a different direction.'

Sue began to refine her education programs and limit her teaching to the local area. She sees it as a blessing to have an optimistic personality. 'You find out who you really are when stuff like that happens in your life and if you're an optimist, that will come through and you'll handle it one day at a time.

'I was still running groups and doing seminars on body image and self-esteem, and one day I thought I'd take Sunny with me because I can demonstrate those ideas clearly with him. When I stand a certain way, Sunny backs away from me – which clearly shows what "no" looks like – and when I drop my shoulders and relax he'll come right in again.

'That day, there was a youth worker there from Wesley Mission and she said that what Sunny and I did was visually powerful and it would be so amazing to show that to the youth. Within two weeks she had every youth coordinator from the schools in the area here, and from then on I've never advertised; I've been fully booked since.

'It took me a while to get the respect of some of the youth organisations. I had to show them that these are practical life skills in how to use your body language, how to control your adrenaline, how to deal with difficult situations and stay calm. I'm teaching effective communication and life skills based on natural horsemanship skills.

'We do horse agility here and we pop them over jumps, all using natural horsemanship skills, and for the kids to be able to do that they have to be really clear with their communication, really calm and focused. We have a show at the end of the course and we have a judge come in and they have to complete the course very calmly, be connected to their horse, and they get ribbons and certificates and trophies at the end. The achievement for these kids is really significant as they've most likely never achieved anything or been praised for anything.

'Natural horsemanship is not about who does something best, it's how you handle something when it goes wrong. When it does go wrong, it's a great opportunity for them to show the judge how they breathe out, relax, start over and get the connection happening again.' Much as Sue had to do in the time after her cancer diagnosis.

Larry's addition to Sue's equine family meant that she had a complete set of four different temperament types, which psychologists label choleric, sanguine, melancholic and phlegmatic. But this was an accident. Sue hadn't been looking to do that. In fact, she'd never even heard those words before. She recognised that she had four distinct personalities and labelled them with each horse's name. It wasn't until she was talking with a psychology researcher that the researcher was able to identify them as each of the four temperament types.

Sunny is choleric, which in humans generally indicates good decision-making abilities, the skill to take instant actions, a strong personality type that can come across as intimidating to Mindys and Larrys. Mindy is melancholic (finds confrontation difficult, generally gets along with everyone, very sensitive and not good at saying no); Yogi is sanguine (enthusiastic, bored easily, often has difficulty in school or in boring jobs – Yogi himself will steal laptops, gumboots and mobile phones, bite timid people, and has difficulty concentrating to the point where Sue describes him as like a child with ADHD); and Larry is phlegmatic (gets along with everyone, dislikes confrontation, good mediators and an aptitude for fine detail).

The therapeutic value in having all four temperaments in her herd means that every client who comes can identify with one of those horses; however, once they identify what type of personality they are, Sue then matches them with the opposite personality type so they see how their behaviours and emotions affect others.

Larry made up the complete set that Sue didn't even know she needed. Now her teaching work could be taken to another level.

And that not only benefitted herself – her horsemanship playing a crucial role in her mindfulness and healing process – but it meant her clients benefitted too. Larry has changed not only Sue's life but, as she says, hundreds of lives.

'What I see with some of the kids who have a problem with aggression is that they bond with Larry like you wouldn't believe. And Larry won't walk with you if you go ahead of him, you have to walk beside him. It's all about being polite and respectful. He's such a dignified little gentleman. And I see all these kids who have such a problem with aggression out there working with Larry softly and gently . . . it just makes me cry. If we didn't have Larry with that personality he's got we wouldn't be reaching those kids like we do. He's so special. He's been the addition here that has really made the team and made it possible to deliver a professional, long-term-results program.

'He's absolutely changed my life. And I tell the kids this all the time. He makes me see that things can happen in the past and you can go through some pretty bad things, but you've got to learn to trust again. Larry's learned to trust again and I think that's a really important lesson because if those kids don't learn to trust again after they've lost trust in other people, then their life will always be about never being able to fully commit to anything. And for me, because I've been through the breast cancer, his message really resonates with me: *that was then, this is now.*

'I say that to the kids. Imagine Larry then and look at him now. He's been through a shocking time. Imagine how traumatised he would have been. He arrived in a truck with cattle and horses, he was pushed down a ramp, and he would have smelt where he was going, into that abattoir, he would have felt the fear, the terror. He couldn't handle a stick or a rope, he was probably being hit and he hadn't been looked after. But he's had to learn to trust again. Not everybody is like that in life and you've got to be wise and suss people out and learn to trust. But be wise about it. That's Larry's great lesson to share.

'These kids have been through such intense trauma. But then they get in there and do their lessons and you see them on show day, out there with Larry in his top hat and bow tie, and they're all puffed out and loving it. That's what it's all about.

'It makes them realise they can be focused, they can be calm and they can be assertive. It's particularly great for girls who've been assaulted, for them to know what it feels like to be extroverted instead of introverted. Introverted body language attracts bullies, so we teach them how to extrovert their body language to keep them safer.

'It's the same with the bullies. If I pair someone with really strong energy with small, sensitive Larry, his little eyes will pop out of his head and his little feet start to run and they say, "What's going on?" and I say, "You're energy's too high, just breathe out," and they do. I teach them how to breathe out and relax their belly so the adrenaline slows down and then Larry will come creeping over and lean against their leg because they've made him feel safe by dropping their energy. And then they realise how good it feels to have someone feel safe instead of scared of them. They're bullies, so they know how to scare people, and this teaches them how to be soft.

'I've had some students here who've been diagnosed as lacking any empathy, and they've worked with Larry and the empathy has just flowed out of them. The bond they've had with him and the softness they've shown has led to some of the diagnoses changing. Just by doing natural horsemanship skills.'

Horses Helping Humans was meant to be a business that focused on women's groups and corporate training. But the youth work became so big so fast that it's kept Sue fully booked. The downside in terms of the business model, though, is that youth groups can't afford to pay much for the training. Sue knew how important it was to keep providing the service and ran the business at a loss for such a long time that she and husband, Craig, refinanced their house two years in a row and were still working another two jobs outside of the business to make ends meet. At this point, Sue says they were exceptionally lucky to have a generous family in Melbourne step up and sponsor the work she was doing so they could keep going.

Finally, they formed a charity that runs alongside the business of Horses Helping Humans. The Horse Whispering Youth Program offers its services to youth programs at discounted rates and the fundraising income makes up the shortfall. Horses Helping Humans will continue to focus on women, private families and corporate training, which helps support the charity work.

Every day brings Sue new cases, stories and referrals.

'I'm like the guy in the circus who has all those plates spinning in the air. That's me, running from one plate to another and back again to make sure none of them fall. Because I don't want any kid to fall. Life's so busy, but so rewarding.'

Sue says her future is a constant work in progress. She gets calls from all over the country asking her if she will travel and whether she'll train other people to use her specific personality profiling system and communication program. She's working on multi-media projects to enable her to travel to schools and workplaces with a really good film and teach her workshops with that.

'I can't be all day every day out in the paddock. I'm not reaching enough people. My motto in life is, and I guess it's my mission statement for what I do, that there should never be any fear or intimidation in communication. There should only be trust and respect. And the amount of bullying that goes on, not just in our schools but in the corporate world, is horrific. I hear more often than I can count stories from people who break down and cry because they have to work with a bully every day and it's affecting their health. So for me to be able to give them tools to go away and start to change the way they think and hold their body language so that they're more empowered is just fantastic.'

It's something Sue is especially passionate about after going through cancer. It's taken her years to work through the anxiety that was left behind after her surgeries. But during those years, she's come to understand herself much better and know where her limits are.

'I have to be careful because it's my personality to take on too much and get too busy. Before the breast cancer I was at the whim of other people and I didn't have good boundaries. That's why I teach that now with the horsemanship because you don't want to wait to go through something huge before you learn to say no. You need to learn to say it *now*. And even though I've been through all that and I still have to work on my anxiety levels, I have a different sort of calmness now that I didn't have back then. That's come from going through that and appreciating different things.'

The need to say no came to Sue in a sudden realisation while going through surgeries.

'It happened when I realised that my immune system needed to stay very healthy. When you say yes to things you really want to say no to, and when you feel intimidated and when you feel guilty, all of that affects your health. You get anxious. You get resentful. You feel scared about saying no to some people. And all of those emotions affect your immune system. I realised I couldn't let people affect my health.

'I still struggle with that. I say yes all the time in the work that I do; I help people and being in that situation will always bring that up. But I know when I'm pushed too far now and I'll say I can't do any more. My boundaries are a lot clearer and my ability to say no has gotten better.

'I didn't know how to say no with my body language before but now I can show people, through the horses, what saying no looks like. And then you do it and it feels really good.

'But I've learned that the hard way. I do remember one young doctor saying to my husband, "Is your wife the sort of person who does everything for everybody?" And Craig said, "Yes." And the doctor said, "Well, that's quite common that women who have that personality type become ill." That was a shock to me. When you do so much for everyone else because you can't say no, and you're tired and stressed . . . I wonder. I just wonder.'

The intense journey Sue's been on has driven her passion to help others make changes in their own lives before it's too late. She says her calling in life is to be able to teach people to communicate more effectively and her horses are the perfect way to do that. By embracing her yearning to move to acreage and reconnect with horses, she's built herself a powerful platform from which to educate others. And she continues to heal herself at the same time through the mindfulness of horsemanship and staying in the present.

'You need to make sure you're respected. Often when we're giving to people we're actually not respected for all that we're giving them. It's learning to step back and say, hang on a moment, is this person really appreciative? Does this person really have the same integrity as me? Do they feel real gratitude for what I'm doing here? There's that old proverb in the Bible: "Don't throw your pearls before the swine." What the pearls represent is your life force, your empathy for people, it's your love, it's your care. And if you keep throwing all that down into the pigpen it will be trampled into the mud.

'Before the cancer diagnosis a lot of people would ring me up with their problems. But going through that, you certainly learn quickly who are your true friends. I started to open my eyes and I came to the understanding that you have to make sure you have respect before you give affection, which is a foundational horsemanship principle.

'It's a huge thing for women to learn how to manage their sensitivity so that it's a positive thing in their life and not a negative. You have to learn to control it. It's like having a power that has to be used in the right way. When working with horses, you have to not let your strength become your weakness, and you want to turn your weakness into your strength. Use it for good but make sure there's plenty left over for other things, like yourself and your family.'

She's come a long way but Sue says her healing journey is still an ongoing process. And recently she took another step forward.

'I used to compete in aerobic competitions and body-shaping competitions. So physicality was a really big part of who I was. It was never about *oh, look at me*, it was about the joy and fun of being on stage.

'After I had the reconstruction I was really embarrassed about my body. And after thirty years in the fitness industry, I'd stopped training. But then I saw this woman come out on stage recently and I suddenly realised I wanted to train again. And I've been training and feeling really good about it.

'I want to get back up on stage. I want to be an inspiration to women who are going to have double mastectomies because you think the whole world is about your breasts. When I had my reconstruction done I did a little postcard up for my surgeon. I'd been saying to him that it was okay for other women going through mastectomies to ring me and come and see me because when I went through it I had no one my age to look at. So I said I was happy to meet with women and a few came around and I showed them what I'd been through. I did up this lovely postcard with a picture of me sitting on Sunny at Cabarita Beach. He's in the water and I'm sitting on him bareback with just shorts and a bikini top on, and I had written on it, "What's life really like after a double mastectomy and reconstruction?" and then on the other side of the postcard it said, "It's just fine."

'The women who were coming to see me were just freaking out about having their breasts off. A couple of them wouldn't go through the surgery, even though they'd been advised to; the thought of losing their breasts was too much. And I just want to say to them, your life is so much more important than your breasts. Life is so much more than that.

'I want to be able to stand up there and say, "Look, you can have awesome arms, awesome legs, an awesome bottom, an awesome stomach and an awesome back!" And at the age of fifty-two it's not all about your boobs. You are more than a pair of boobs. It's like I'm back. It's like the real me has been too embarrassed or too guilty but no, I'm back. And I'll be standing there with a double bicep pose in a bling-bling bikini while Aerosmith's "Back in the Saddle" blasts through the room.'

Alongside this powerful message runs another, equally powerful one that Sue says she wants every single person who comes to her place to take away with them: 'Animals everywhere have feelings and personalities. You'd be surprised how many people don't believe that. But it's so clear. And maybe when they leave here they'll be nicer to another animal out there and change another animal's life. That's another one of Larry's gifts to world – opening hearts and passing on that message.'

SALTY

Through the Boer War and World World I, Australia sent around 180 000 horses overseas to serve in the battles. The Waler, a breed named for its origins in New South Wales, possessed sturdy physicality and an admired temperament, and was the predominant breed to go over the seas and carry the men who served their country. As history tells it, only one of those 180 000 horses came home. The rest were shot or simply released to fend for themselves.

Today, Walers are still highly sought-after as riding horses, able to survive tough Australian conditions and loved for their personable attributes and their historical connection to our Light Horse brigades. But many of the original Waler descendants live as wild horses across our deserts. They are considered feral pests and are therefore subject to aerial culling. (Just recently, in May 2013, 10 000 horses were marked to be culled by aerial shooting at Tempe Downs Station in the Northern Territory.)

Salty was a descendent of these Walers. She lived a free life in her herd at Newhaven, a cattle station three hundred and fifty kilometres north-west of Alice Springs until the property was sold to a conservation group and became a wildlife sanctuary. When that happened, all the horses had to go. The horses were identified as pure Waler stock – a unique find. They escaped aerial culling but were instead captured and taken to saleyards in Alice Springs, a common process for dealing with mass numbers of horses in a timely manner. As a result, most were sold for slaughter for pet food, but a few rescue groups from around the country managed to save a handful.

One of those who found a new home was Salty, a young pregnant grey mare, who made the enormous journey (more than three thousand kilometres) from the hot red desert centre of Australia all the way to the chilly green mountains of Tasmania.

Scilla Sayer lives in Tasmania and works in therapy, education and recreation with people and horses. Scilla met Salty via a friend of a friend, Trudi Young, who had bought three of the rescued Walers – a stallion and two pregnant mares – from the Newhaven station. One mare slipped her foal (miscarried) and the other, Salty, carried hers to full term and raised him. But circumstances changed for Trudi and she had to rehome her horses.

'Trudi adored Salty and had heard about the horse connection work I do,' says Scilla, 'so she asked me if I would take Salty to see if there was any way I could reduce the intensity of her flight response and then find her a home. I told her that I don't offer retraining and selling-on, but after sensing the depth of love and concern in Trudi's voice, I said Salty could come for six weeks with no promises of any sort of result or outcome.'

At the time, Salty was agisted at a training facility that had a focus on transforming thoroughbred racehorses into eventers.

'I couldn't work effectively with her there as she was paddocked on her own and this was clearly alien and distressing for a herd horse like her. So I requested that she come home to my property, which is in the bush, very private, and where she would have the companionship of a number of other horses. I went up to the training centre to bring her home, but she was anxious about the horse float, claustrophobic and terrified of anything being around her hind legs. Any kind of entrapment was devastating for her.'

Scilla would have preferred to spend a lot of time with Salty, building her trust and gently desensitising her to the float (a completely unnatural and terrifying object for an animal of prey as they have no escape route), but she didn't have the time. Salty had to get on the float in order to move to Scilla's place.

'My heart ached for the grief I felt this little mare was experiencing. She was both homeless and herdless. But two and a half hours after we met, she accepted my leadership and we made it home safely. When she got here, she backed off really calmly, looked around and took a deep breath, like she'd come home. And that was how we began our journey together.

'She was about five years old, 14.1 hands high, and quite plain, like most of her family – straight face, white with little blue flecks. Within about a week of her being here, I knew she would stay. I bought her for the price paid to bring her down from the Northern Territory. Her presence was so beautiful. She was so gentle.'

Salty was already named when she came to Scilla.

'The names of many Walers refer to places where the Light Horse saw action. She was named after Es Salt, a city in Jordan whose capture was led by mounted Australian troops. And I thought "Salty" was an appropriate name for her colouring too.'

Scilla lives at 'Wrenshaven', twenty-one acres of bush in Leslie Vale, near Hobart in Tasmania, in the foothills of Mount Wellington, towards Huonville.

'It's not classic horse country at all, but good for ponies prone to laminitis or becoming overweight.'

She has two sons, both of whom were passionate three-day event riders in their teens and early twenties. Now married with their own families, Scilla has become 'Granny GG', in recognition of her connection with horses. Until recently, Scilla's mother, Mary, also lived with her for half of each year to escape the Scottish winters. But Mary passed away last year.

Scilla was born in Edinburgh, Scotland. Her earliest memories of being with horses are of being with her maternal grandmother's Highland pony, Blossom. Her large extended family would visit her grandparents 'up the glen' in Perthshire. Blossom was a Garron, a stocky type of Highland pony breed.

'She was a big, strong, white mare who was used for deer-stalking, pulling, trekking and everything else.'

Scilla was in her late thirties when she came to Australia, a move influenced by the politics in Britain at that time and the disharmony in her marriage, which contributed to the couple's efforts to find a fresh start.

'Tasmania was the part I was most attracted to. It's very similar to Scotland in a lot of ways. And it opened the door for me to have horses here because it was more affordable. In the UK there's no way you can afford to do what people manage here.'

Scilla's work is deeply rooted in spirituality and philosophy.

She works in two different fields: helping horses themselves, through a collection of natural horsemanship–based techniques; and helping people.

'I'm a teacher by my initial qualifications. I believe that learning and development with people is actually about drawing out what is already there. If we're sensitive and aware we can encourage the knowledge we already have to emerge and blossom. And I feel that very strongly with horses too. I'm not there to educate them, except to help "lead them out", which is what the Latin word, *educare*, means. I learned that some time ago, and it filled me with inspiration because that's exactly what we do. We don't fill people up; we encourage the knowledge that is innately there to grow.

'While I've watched and learned from a lot of different horse trainers, I don't follow any particular system or have a "guru". I don't have a specific leading light in my spiritual life or in my equine-focused life because I see the horses themselves as my teachers and every time I'm with them I learn more. If I just stop and listen and watch, usually they'll tell me what else they need. I try and *listen* to them; I don't try and *whisper* to them. "Horse whispering" is anthropocentric and I'd rather be equicentric.

'I work in the space between people and horses. That's a broad enough umbrella under which I can put a number of things. I help people with their horses when they encounter a particular problem such as going into a float, separation anxiety, rushing or pushing, etcetera. I work with children and adults who are struggling with anxiety, self-esteem, the confines of the education system or the impact of trauma from physical or mental illness. And I work with people in a more overtly spiritual space with horses, using yoga, tai chi and mindfulness practices in the company of horses.'

Much of Scilla's life in Australia has been spent with people who need support.

'My primary commitment was to children who had suffered abuse and neglect. And for some of those children, having contact with horses was what kept them going through their adolescence. I extended my training into welfare and counselling and was drawn to working in child protection as a case manager, senior practice consultant and policy officer for eighteen years.'

Her background as a teacher, as well as her lengthy role in child protection services here in Australia, gives her a firm foundation for her work today. Exploring the relatively new realm of equine-facilitated therapy and learning, she completed training in New Zealand, America and Australia. Now she works with students by giving them life skills to thrive in education and to transition out of school; girls and women with eating disorders; adults with a range of complex issues; and with newly arrived refugees, including young boys who have been soldiers in war zones.

'To see these young African men working with a woman, for a start, and then working with Salty where there was no permission for violence or aggression of any kind, was absolutely fascinating. It softened and opened up those boys in ways that were truly amazing and very humbling.

When her marriage ended, Scilla found herself in a position to totally focus on what was important to her: deepening her relationship with horses, exploring natural horsemanship techniques and various equine-facilitated learning techniques, strengthening her spiritual work and devoting her life to the path she felt she was called to follow.

'Over the past decade, hundreds of people have described the sense of "haven" they feel when they come to Wrenshaven. I'm not interested in promoting to corporate clients, even though I have done some delightful team-building days with community-based organisations with the help of the horses. Mostly my clients don't have very much money and these are the people I choose to work with. I don't have an arena. I have a sand-covered circular clearing in the bush, defined by the logs from the trees that once stood in that space. We work and play where we can and try to remain in nature as much as possible.'

That connection to nature is what made Scilla and Salty's relationship extra special. She was a true brumby, born and raised in the wild, untouched by humans. All natural horsemanship theories are based on wild horse behaviour, and all of Scilla's practices are based on working with a horse in the way that honours its natural behaviours. To have an authentically wild horse in her midst was a unique gift.

'Watching her taught me about true herd behaviour and true wildness. Salty was such a perfect model of the gentle, respected lead mare, a well-adjusted mother horse in a well-adjusted herd. People often came and brought new horses (with problems) into the mix and they watched them express their strengths and their insecurities in a herd. The bossy ones challenged the existing leadership patterns and balance had to be re-established. Salty became an amazing balancing influence in any group. She did a lot of healing of other horses simply by having clear, quiet boundaries as well as patient acceptance. She taught them horse manners.'

These were manners learned while running wild in the Northern Territory, where a horse's wisdom and behaviour could mean the difference between life and death.

'I feel her heart was broken when she was taken away from her herd, and her herd was destroyed. She was always acutely aware of the movement of horses on and off my property. She wouldn't fret, but she would notice and look and watch. It was a really deep mothering quality in her.'

And Salty's nurturing tendencies extended to people too.

'I'm a grandmother of two beautiful children so far, and four-year-old Poppy is already inheriting the love of horses from her parents and elders. We play a combination of fairies and ponies most weeks when I have the pleasure of her company for the day. Salty was without doubt her favourite. I will never forget the day when Poppy was walking around the edge of the pony play area, wearing one of her lovely fairy dresses and balancing on the logs that edge the sandy arena. Salty, totally at liberty, kept watch and followed her around and stopped whenever Poppy did and moved on quietly when Poppy decided to progress.'

Scilla identifies as a Quaker, and it is a connection that has supported her throughout her life at critical transition points, such as the end of her marriage and her resignation from child protection work.

'The thing that Quakers hold true to is non-violence – whatever you perceive to be non-violent. I would hope that my communication with horses is non-violent. It doesn't mean that there aren't times when I am very determined and clear. I don't think anyone who works with horses could say they never use strength and clarity to get a point across. Non-violence, respect, humility and listening are all Quaker principles. Alternatives to violence are accessed through stopping, breathing and reflecting rather than rushing into a crisis.

'There are many parallels with how we work with horses. Instead of jumping in to solve a problem, we can step back from the horse and say, "Do whatever you have to do. I'm going to stay here, look out for my own safety and try to keep you safe. When you have released the tension you are holding and are able to return to connection with me, can we explore how we can move onward together again?" It's a process of enquiry and I think that process means you are always learning. I try to take that to the work I do with horses.'

Salty's innate wildness gave Scilla the chance to apply these Quaker principles on a daily basis.

'She taught me so much about herds. I just learned and learned and learned from her. I didn't know what I was going to do about her "dangerous flight response" (the reason she came to me in the first place) because I feel that horses *need* that flight response and that it is *us* who need to be able to deal with how that behaviour is acted out, not them. I didn't ever want her to have a bit in her mouth again and I wanted to give her a different kind of ridden experience if she was to ever to carry a human again.

'I used to ride my other horse, Sam, and lead her out. Initially she wouldn't go beside him. She'd either stay behind him or rush to the front. When I thought about her as a herd horse, I surmised that was because she was being a respectful younger mare who didn't know quite where she fitted in the complex social system of the herd. As a member of a herd you earn the right to go alongside another horse when you are accepted into equity with them.'

Understanding wild horse behaviour is key to Scilla's work as a 'problem solver' for 'difficult' horses.

'Salty repeatedly heightened my awareness about how we ask horses to do things that are truly so hard for them. And we make it even more difficult by rushing them with more pressure or demands, rather than stopping and saying, "Right, if you were in the wild now, what would you do? How would you survive?"

'I remember the first day I actually sat on her. I'd taken her for a ride, again beside Sam, and they'd reached the point where they were prepared to canter together. I was so proud of Sam because he would wait until I'd encouraged her to canter and then he would canter and I felt so privileged because it was like I was part of the herd. She helped us to have that melding of beings. That's so rare.

'She felt really wise but so fragile at the same time. I always respected her as a horse but I also say that she was my soul companion. For me, she was the most special being in the herd, but you wouldn't necessarily notice her first in the group because she was not "flashy", and we often had a little Arab mare who looks very similar to her from a distance. A lot of people got them muddled up, or were drawn more to the Arab, Sula, as she is much more pretty-pretty, with a dishy face, big dark eyes and the characteristic Arab flowing mane and tail, while Salty didn't. But Sula is more ditzy and the other horses tend to push her out to the perimeter of the group. If they'd been in the wild together, the cougars would have caught her and eaten her long before they caught Salty.

'When she needed to, she would be assertive with a difficult horse. She reformed a lot of horses and ponies with "complex behaviours", who, like people with similar labels, came to my home. A beautiful Arab named Indi was known as "the black bitch" as she would chase people out of the paddock and bite dogs and threaten other horses. She was thrown out of the paddock where she was agisted and her owner asked if she could come and join the herd at Wrenshaven for a bit. Once in with the horses, she took the water, she took the nice places, she isolated and dominated the vulnerable pony and then expected to be fed first by any human who approached the paddock. Salty and Sam went right off to the other side of the field, not prepared to waste any effort in dealing with this behaviour. Indi found herself totally isolated. But twenty-four hours later, I found Salty lying down right beside Indi. It was such a beautiful example of compassion and acceptance by her and it was really after that that Indi's behaviour began to change completely and she was able to be in a herd. Indi is now a well-seasoned and wonderful therapy horse.

'Salty gave me incredible insight every day on the functioning of a herd – which we can only ever *glimpse* with a domesticated herd. But with her as the lead mare, I could observe the subtle dynamics of the equine community and how critical it was to the balance of the group to have a mare with the characteristics of a horse like Salty. Bossy, insecure mares will push, threaten, distract and dominate. Salty epitomised non-violent communication in the paddock.'

Not long after Scilla agreed to tell Salty's story as part of this book, her beloved soul partner passed from this world at only ten years of age. Scilla was at the spiritual community of Findhorn in Scotland at the time, a place she says was the perfect place to be if she could not physically be with Salty at the time of her death.

It's not completely clear what caused Salty's illness. It was described as cardio-toxicity but there was a lot of confusion between the vets.

'It's possible that her heart was already compromised in some way – physically or psychologically – and then it is possible that she was affected by a virus or had eaten something that gave her a toxic reaction. The symptoms were stumbling, falling, seizures, not eating, and clearly being very miserable. It was difficult for the person who was caring for her while I was away. She had a lot of conflicting advice being given to her and I wasn't easily contactable because I was on the other side of the world with intermittent internet connection.'

As she became weaker, Salty was separated from the other horses, including her best friend, Sam, on the advice of the vets. But as the time of her passing grew nearer, the person looking after her in Scilla's absence put her back with them. Back with her herd once more, she lay down and died.

'I struggle with the guilt of not being with her but by the time we realised she wasn't going to recover it was too late for me to have made it home to be with her. She would have died before I even got to the airport.

'She was sick for about a week, from when it started to when she died. My mum was also sick for a week before she died. And they didn't really know why my mum died, either. Just like Salty. Rightly, or wrongly, I just thank God they could both die on their own terms.

After Scilla returned, she visited Salty's grave on her friend's property.

'We planted five little silver birch trees. Salty loved silver birches and the colour is right for her. And the number five represents the five horses that were there with her when she passed.

'I don't think it does us any harm to really deeply grieve and really hurt. So many people have said how Salty was their favourite in the therapy herd. I never owned this little mare, I only had custodianship of her for a brief time and wish often that I could have done that better.

'She always gave me the feeling that she was an old soul who entered the human sphere to look after people. If there was no human to attend to, she'd find a goat or a calf and look after it. She was deeply maternal. I always felt she mourned for her herd and she also pined for another foal. She reminded me of the girls I've worked with over the years who have had babies in their teens. Salty was so young herself, only three, when she had her foal. I have a photo somewhere of her when she arrived in Tasmania. In it, she's a bewildered-looking little thing, with her head down and her big tummy swelling way out behind her narrow chest. She was just like a fifteen-year-old pregnant girl.'

Scilla has had to process not just one major loss in Salty, but also the passing of her mother just months earlier.

'My mum was an artist and after both she and Salty passed away, I found a painting that she'd done a couple of years before. Mum wasn't particularly emotionally connected to horses but she loved Salty. Here she had caught in watercolour a glimpse of the little mare in among the rose bushes at Wrenshaven. Salty would eat all the things she needed around the garden, like the rosehips, and I loved to have her wandering around the house.

'After Mum died, I had a memorial ceremony for her here in the garden and the horses were in the paddock next to where we were sitting in a circle around a small stone labyrinth. People who knew and loved Mum were sitting quietly around the edge of the circular stone path and Salty was the only horse that came over to join us. She was undoubtedly part of that ceremony. And when it was all finished she waited until everyone had returned to the house for afternoon tea. It was only a short time afterwards that I said goodbye to her and left for three months overseas, never to see her again.

Scilla says that Salty's biggest gift to her was to learn more about wild horses than ever before and to really experience what it must be like to live in a herd, acting on instinct, and then trying to work with a human being, who is the total opposite. But she says she's also been given the gift of letting go, which is a process, and takes time.

'I miss her beyond words. Looking at the painting of her done by a loving friend, and the little altar on which her tail hair rests with rainbow ribbons intertwined through it, and the photo of Poppy and her at the arena, brings up such sadness. But I don't hold on to her and I'm now having to let go of many other things in my life too. I know she'll be there for the next step I take in my life purpose, whatever that is, just in a different way.

'I share with her the broken-heartedness of leaving my herd and hence I travel back to Scotland when I can. I am not going to take on any more horses, not for a while anyway, because I need to be able to feel free to travel and possibly to write a book, for which Salty is undoubtedly an inspiration. I need time, space and freedom to do that.

'I treasure Salty's memory and I gain as much, if not more, from her now than I did when she was alive. But you can't feel deep grief if you can't feel deep love. In affluent cultures like Australia, we're very fortunate to have the luxury of "falling in love" with our horses and not having to put them in a cart and use them as tools until they are no longer viable, when we either eat them ourselves or feed them to our dogs. But with that gift of relationship comes a huge responsibility to truly honour what they have to teach us.

'The last time I saw her alive, she was peacefully eating on a southern Tasmanian hillside with Sam. Shortly after I left, a friend captured on camera the rays of a late summer rainbow falling gently onto Salty. Her passing has set me free, personally, to continue my journey of life purpose, perhaps elsewhere and in new ways. The same gift was given by my mum's passing and I feel that these two beloved beings are connected in some way I can never fully understand. They both experienced loss of freedom in their lives, found refuge in Tasmania, then brought so much joy and insight to the many people drawn to the place. I'm not yet sure what lies ahead. For now, it feels like the time for the shedding of skins, patterns and even identities in order for creative change to occur.

'As summer and winter solstices coincided in Scotland and Australia, my equine mate became pure soul and my life made a profound shift. I am grateful each day for the blessing of having had her beauty and wisdom touch me in ways that are both boundless and enduring.'

HORSES I HAVE KNOWN AND LOVED

The first time I rescued a horse I was fourteen years old, but I didn't realise at the time that Hercules was a rescue. It was only more than twenty years later, after I'd created a horse rescue charity in south-east Queensland, and I saw firsthand how the lifecycle of most horses went – especially racehorses – that I came to see it for what it was.

On that day, I sat in the car beside Dad and fidgeted, a soup of nervous excitement in my belly. The drive seemed to take forever; every set of traffic lights turned red and made me wait just that little bit longer to meet my horse for the first time.

I'd been waiting for a horse since I was five.

Mum always said that I'd inherited the horse obsession from her mother. My dad's family liked horses – but only if they were racing around a track and winning them money. But my earliest memories of longing for a horse were always associated with my maternal grandmother.

Nanna's house in Nundah backed onto bushland, with a

trickling creek that wound its way along the border of her property. As far back as I could remember, there was always at least one horse tethered to a long rope eating grass down in that creek. Visits to Nanna became punctuated by a walk in the late afternoon to retrieve the horses and bring them back to the house. Nanna would throw me up onto the bare back of a horse. The smell of its body, the warmth of its skin beneath my legs, the feel of its rough mane clenched in my tiny hands, the power in its muscles, filled me with such a strong sense of connection.

Where the other girls at school covered their textbooks with pictures of movie stars and pop icons, I cut out pictures of horses – horses lazing in fields, jumping coloured obstacles in competitions, dancing in dressage, swimming in creeks, barrel racing in western gear, mustering cattle in the dust. I glued them all carefully to my books. The girls at school talked about boys and wrote 'I love Michael' and 'David Rulz!' on their notepads. I wrote 'I love horses'. They spent their Saturdays shopping in the Queen Street Mall for lipsticks and shoes. I spent mine at a local riding school in jodhpurs, with dirt under my fingernails and sweat on my shirt.

I'd obsessed about owning a horse for as long as I could remember. And finally, it was happening.

Anxiously, I watched the streetlights pass us by, listened to the *tick-tock* of the blinker as we turned corners and silently begged my dad to go faster. We cruised past the tall walls of the racetrack.

'Nearly there,' Dad said, smiling.

Dad and his brother owned a racehorse, which resided at a training stable at Deagon, not far from the two racetracks of Eagle Farm and Doomben. By word of mouth, the trainer had heard of a racehorse in a neighbouring training stable, just a little down the road, that was looking for a home.

The car slowed and pulled to the side of the road. I took a deep breath that caught in my chest over the fluttering of my heart. I stepped down the long, dirt driveway towards the stables, Dad at my side.

Previously, when I'd visited Dad's racehorse at the stables, there had always been a flurry of activity: horses were tethered to motorised clotheslines, walking in circles to keep fit, as if on treadmills; stable hands carried buckets of food to waiting horses; or a farrier might be heard nailing a horseshoe. But this time, all was quiet. It was a clear, still day in October, a Sunday afternoon. And there was no one around.

My eyes scanned the grounds, anticipating where my horse could be. And then I saw him. A white horse, bigger than any I'd ever ridden before, paced furiously in his stable. He stopped his circuit briefly as he heard us crunching on the dirt and poked his head out over the stable door. He had a perfect face – big black eyes set dramatically against his white face, a long, silvery grey forelock that hung well below his eye level, a dark-skinned muzzle with a pink snip, and small, curious ears that pointed directly at us.

'If that's my horse, I'll die.'

This horse was the most beautiful animal I'd ever seen. He was a fairytale.

The trainer came lumbering out from behind a stable. 'Brian, is it?' He lunged towards my dad and shook his hand.

'Hi. This is my daughter, Joanne.'

He nodded. 'Well, he's in here.' He turned to the stable with the big white horse and unlatched the half-door. I could barely stand still as he slipped a halter over the horse's head and clipped a lead rope to him, the smell of wet sawdust pungent in the air.

The door swung wide. The trainer led him outside. The horse stood to his full height, watching me out of the corner of his eye.

'He's beautiful,' I said. I looked over his body, mostly white with dark dapples of grey, concentrating around the points on his legs, his rump and his neck, dark skin showing on his nose, and a silver mane. In his summer coat, his hair was so fine that I could see his black skin beneath it and I could see the brand on his left shoulder, the number three indicating that he was born in 1983. I looked down at his feet to see that he had no shoes on.

'Doesn't he need shoes?' I asked.

The trainer fidgeted with the pockets in his pants and looked at the ground. 'Ah, yes, he does actually.'

In the corner of my mind was a vague observation that his feet looked a little spongy. I let the thought pass, captivated by this horse's presence and beauty.

Dad looked at me. 'I think we'll be taking him,' he said.

I nodded quickly.

'Great.' The trainer smiled.

I let their conversation fade into the background. I stroked the long neck of my horse, feeling the warmth of his body beneath my hand. I had my first real horse. And to me, he was perfect.

Hercules was almost 17 hands high and a stocky sort of Thoroughbred. In certain poses his features harked back to the Arabian ancestry floating in all Thoroughbred blood. But unlike the general hardiness of Arabian horses, Thoroughbreds aren't built to last. They are bred to race hard for a handful of years, and are in training years before they're fully grown or have a complete set of adult teeth. Their careers are short, leaving easily twenty or more years ahead of them. But what happens to them after the racecourse is rarely considered in the breeding and it's a sad fact that the majority end up in slaughter yards.

The internet wasn't around when I met Hercules. There were no websites or social media sites to throw pictures in my face of the dark side of the world. To me, the whispers of 'the glue factory' were rumours.

Hercules was just one more ex-racehorse out of the tens of thousands that are bred each year. He was a gelding, with no prospects of breeding, was carrying injuries, had appalling hoof health (as my instincts had tried to warn me), and showed no tendencies towards dressage, pony club, mustering or show jumping – nothing competitive that would make him 'worth' anything. As fortune would have it, he had a particularly lovely nature and it was likely this that had prompted some effort by the racing stable to find him a home rather than simply calling the dogger to come and collect him for a few hundred dollars in cash, as would have been easier to do.

I spent sixteen years with Hercules and stuck with him through chronic hoof problems and recurring eye conditions, all of which were expensive, painful, long-lasting and logistically difficult to deal with. He had numerous falls. Colic. Laminits and founder. Hoof abscesses. And, his final nemesis, Cushing's disease, an autoimmune condition that eventually took him from me in the form of an infection he was unable to fight and resulted in cardio-vascular collapse.

With enormous grief, I allowed the vet to euthanase him under a tall gum tree, and buried him there.

The emptiness of the paddock in the weeks that followed were nothing compared to the emptiness in my heart where my giant horse had resided for so long. I had stuck with him long past the point most others would have, because I knew with every one of my cells that his life was important and he had a right to live it with love. When an animal entered my life it became a part of the family and we would battle through whatever challenge came our way. He had been my constant companion, adventurer, friend, teacher and reason to get out of bed in the morning – to traipse to the paddock on cold frosty dawns to feed and rug and pat and whisper.

After his death, I felt like I might never get another horse but, as had been apparent since I was a small child, I was enchanted by them. For me, having a horse wasn't just a whim; it was a lifelong commitment. A non-negotiable *need*.

And that led me to Jum Jum.

Jum Jum (pronounced 'Yum Yum') was a four-year-old part-Arab mare, barely handled, rather thin and pregnant. She was part of an Arabian horse stud that was closing down and the horses were part of a 'fire sale', something I came to learn much more about while officially rescuing horses. I would frequently receive a request for help from someone who had a large property with scores of horses, many unhandled, who had to suddenly sell off everything due to a financial, family or personal crisis. The horses were in tremendous danger of ending up in the one place that would guarantee a cash sale: the abattoir.

And as I was to experience in my efforts to help them, it is very hard to sell or rehome unhandled horses of no particular breeding or colour. (Horses of colour, such as paints, palominos or buckskins, would generally find homes, even if they had no other qualities to recommend them, simply because they were 'prettier' than the standard bay, brown, chestnut or grey horse . . . though a 'home' certainly didn't guarantee happiness.) In hindsight, Jum Jum and her growing baby were rather fortunate to end up in our hands. And Alwyn and I were thrilled to have her, for no other reason than we felt a connection with her.

Her foal, Leila, was born in the early hours of a full moonlit night in September, a perfect, steaming, strong, gorgeous three-quarter Arabian filly that landed in my arms with a splash and a hiccup and filled me with intense joy. And I knew at that moment she would never leave me. None of my horses ever would.

At that time, a lovely white Arabian gelding, Traveller (Trav), was living with us on agistment. When his owner couldn't afford to have him with us any more, I asked if I could lease him, as I didn't have a riding horse. And not long after that, we moved properties and Trav officially came with us as our own horse. Since then, I've had a few offers from people to buy Trav but he is unequivocally not going anywhere.

The next horse to join us was Lincoln, the first official rescue. I agonised about formally adopting him from the charity because we had previously set the limit at three horses and it felt like such a huge commitment – which it was, of course. But once I realised Lincoln and I were simply 'meant' to be together, and accepted the increase in our herd numbers, it opened the gates, and rescue pony Sparky followed, taking our total to five.

Next in line was Anastasia. By this time, I'd made a policy that the charity wouldn't deal with doggers directly. We were too open to being taken advantage of because they knew we'd pay high prices to save a life and they used it to financial gain. We decided it was still okay to go to auctions because it was more of a level playing field there.

But, silly me, I looked at a Facebook page that had photos of horses sitting in the dogger's holding yard and my heart was captured by a flea-bitten grey mare. According to the dogger, she was an ex clerk-of-the-course horse and in her late teens. It was just like it was when I'd received that email about the riding school horses that had been sent to the sales and I made a snap decision to go and save one. I had a tremendous, visceral reaction at the grave injustice of an animal giving its life to the racing industry only to be thrown away at the end. I began to cry and couldn't stop. The dogger wanted six hundred dollars for her, which was ridiculous as a market value, but I didn't care. My heart was taken (which is, of course, what they rely on).

I decided to rescue her myself, personally, outside of the charity. I went into it with my eyes open, and a friend of mine went to collect her for me the next day. When Jane arrived at the dogger's with her four-year-old daughter, the mare was standing in the yards with an array of body parts of horses that had already been slaughtered.

I called our sixth horse Anastasia, which means 'resurrected'. She is likely well into her twenties, and has terrible ligament issues in her legs. She's very weak in her limbs, almost straight through the hocks, and limps terribly when she first gets up from the ground until she warms up. I've had my vet X-ray her worst fetlock but there is no sign of an old break and not much arthritis either. It's unclear what the problem is but it seems to originate in the soft tissues. My vet thinks she has quarter horse in her, and she's very quiet and obviously has a lot of life experience. It's possible that in her previous life she was simply worked too hard for too long and suffered as a result.

But for all her issues, she has strong opinions and is tenacious about them, and shows no sign of wanting to leave this earthly plane.

I wrote an article about Anastasia for the charity's website and newsletter, and for a small equine magazine, just saying how I felt about her, and I received more feedback on that article than on anything else I'd ever written. She's touched many lives through that story.

*

WISDOM THROUGH THE AGES

I think when it comes down to it, most of us seek to feel safe, loved and valued. And I believe animals are looking for the same thing too, especially in old age.

When my grandmother died, I felt such profound loss, not just of her and our relationship, but of her knowledge. All the things I ever thought I might ask, every story I never heard, every bit of wisdom not shared was gone.

Lately, I've been appreciating being 'in the moment' with my older animals – my cat, Jasmine, of fifteen years, and my horse, Anastasia, of unknown years but undoubtedly a great many. Anastasia, in particular, seems to be coming towards the end of her grand life – a life I've known for only a year.

I rescued Anastasia from death in August 2010. She was set to be slaughtered for, what I can only assume, were reasons pertaining to her age. When my friend, Jane, picked Anastasia up from the slaughterhouse holding yard, body parts from her fellow equine friends lay scattered on the ground. Anastasia was next in line. It's a fate I see and hear about all too frequently.

Why do people abandon their aged animals right when the animal needs them to stand up for them the most?

People have their reasons, such as that the horse is of 'no use' any more, or because of finances. It's true that Anastasia costs more to care for than my young horses. I support her joints with supplements and her immune system with herbs. And as she is less mobile than the others, she tends to hang around the house so I can feed her from the shed, rather than foraging with the others.

But what I get back from Anastasia is unquantifiable. For those who believe that a horse needs to have 'a use', I would argue that aged horses have a tremendous amount to offer. They're generally more patient and less reactive (therefore less likely to injure a child). They're generally less active and therefore less likely to break down fences or be a nuisance. They have a lifetime of experience that makes them wonderful for nervous adults and children alike.

Perhaps more importantly, they also offer us the chance to appreciate life in all its stages, teaching us to see beauty and value at any age. What a wonderful gift to teach our children! What wonderful lessons to share about commitment and honour and relationships.

And wouldn't it be nice to think that when we're old and needing extra support that others might see the same value in us as well?

In a culture obsessed by youth and vigour, our aged populations all too often get the short end of the stick. Animals reflect back to us so much about ourselves and if we have a throw-away attitude about our aged animals, then chances are we might have the same attitude about our aged people too. (And you know what they say . . . what goes around, comes around.)

In my work, I often receive emails or phone calls about an aged horse that is no longer any use and that the person wishes to give away or send to slaughter. They ask me, exasperated, 'But what else can I do with it?' I take a deep breath before gently suggesting that perhaps they might consider loving it and caring for it for the rest of its life. (I've yet to have the person change their mind, and so I then do my best to help rehome the horse.)

Anastasia may be heading towards crossing over, but I couldn't feel more honoured to be sharing this phase of life with her. She approaches each day with patience, acceptance and wisdom. She knows how to look after herself; she knows how to manage her physical limitations (without complaint); and she is a reservoir of unimaginable life experience. All that wisdom that is there, just waiting for us to take the time to listen to.

Our home is truly more rich and blessed to have had Anastasia in it.

My wish for the senior animals of the world is that they are honoured, loved and cherished in their later life, just as we all hope we will be one day too.

*

For a long time towards the end of the charity's life, Alwyn and I had two foster horses with us – Bella and Tansy. They had come together from the same rescue, also from a dogger sale. Bella was a brown Shetland pony who was covered in a horrible skin condition. I had no idea what it was but the vet quickly identified it as Queensland itch. I'd never seen anything like it before and learned how very difficult it is to treat. Though I tried every lotion, potion and remedy under the sun, for her, really the only answer was to be rugged continuously throughout the warmer months. Even then, her little ears, one of the few bits exposed, would still suffer terribly.

Bella also had all her top front teeth missing for an unknown reason, and she was sold as being in foal. Time showed, however, that her top teeth had just taken a very long time to come down; she was only two years old and a scan revealed she wasn't pregnant at all.

I really loved Bella. Many foster horses passed through our property and I fell in love with most of them and considered keeping all of them, but Bella really broke my heart. She was a very timid, gentle horse. She took a long time to think about things. She was really tolerant of procedures, needles, hoof-trimming and vets. And she and fellow Shetland Sparky were wonderful companions.

I will always remember the first time Sparky saw Bella. He stopped dead in his tracks and stared at her, face to face. It was almost like he couldn't believe there was another small horse in the world just like him.

Alwyn and I discussed for a long time whether or not to keep Bella. But we felt we'd reached our limit financially, and the last thing we wanted was to become one of the people I'd regularly heard from who had too many horses and suddenly had to get rid of them all because of some sort of personal crisis, which invariably put the horses in jeopardy. Bella made me come hard up against the notion of limits and the idea that 'over-rescuing' could be as much a problem as not rescuing at all.

We also felt that if we were to commit to Bella then we should also commit to Tansy. I can't explain the logic in that; it was just how we felt. But doing so would have taken our personal herd to eight horses and we definitely knew we couldn't do that.

I'd gone head-to-head with the dogger at the saleyards to bid for Tansy. He had his eye on her and all other bidders dropped out quite early, leaving just me and him with our bidding cards in the air. Alwyn stood beside me, urging me on, his eye on the dogger.

'Again, again,' he said. 'Keep going.'

For whatever reason, this particular horse was not leaving on that dogger's truck at the end of the day, not if we had anything to do with it. The dogger scrutinised her body carefully, mentally assessing what she was worth to him in meat dollars, then bowed out at just over four hundred.

Tansy was a ten-year-old ex-racehorse. A man came up to me after we'd bought her at the auction and told me that he'd picked her up on the truck and brought her to the saleyards.

'She's a really nice horse,' he said, with just enough emphasis to suggest he was glad she was saved. 'She's got seedy toe, though.'

Yes, she did. I spent weeks dealing with her seedy toe. I got the vet to take X-rays, I soaked her feet, and eventually my vet cut away all the rotten hoof and filled the holes with a synthetic binding material. Then I spent day after day sitting on the ground at her feet, painting them with iodine, changing dressings and fitting her into rubber boots to walk around in in the paddock. And I thought many times how grateful I was that man had been right and she was indeed a really nice horse.

But that wasn't all of her problems. She also has equine narcolepsy – she falls asleep at random, odd times. And she has an old tendon injury in one of her front legs, which she aggravated badly one day galloping across the paddocks with her best friend, Lincoln, and means she won't tolerate being ridden. But bigger than that was the problem of her neglected parrot mouth, a condition of a severe overbite that means the back molars don't align properly and neither do the front ones. As a result, her top front teeth had grown down so far that they were dead and shaped like daggers, with points on the end. And the last molars at the back of her mouth had done the same, with no opposing tooth to stop them from growing. It was like a horror show in her mouth.

Sadly, parrot mouth can be treated and managed if it's done early enough. I can only assume that, as a racehorse destined for a short working career, the owners saw no need to invest that kind of money into her when she would, in all likelihood, simply be slaughtered anyway.

Tansy was on the charity's books for a long time and had a couple of people interested in her but nothing that panned out. She was a daunting prospect, with her front teeth likely to fall out at some point and therefore a lengthy financial commitment of hard feeding for her for the rest of her life, plus her tendon injury and her narcolepsy.

Then came Oscar.

He was a two-year-old miniature stallion when he arrived, bursting with hormones and frustration, and the only word I could use to describe him was 'insane'! The reason he was surrendered was because the previous owners were moving house and couldn't find a home for him. A stallion with wild behaviours was again a pretty typical sight at dogger auctions, with loads of ungelded colts and stallions in the yards.

I booked him in for gelding as soon as possible but, as we were in a small town, the surgery days were limited and I had to wait a very long and frustrating two weeks for that to happen. (As it was, the vet could barely get him sedated because he was so difficult.) We actually built a post-and-rail fence in his yard just for him because he would dig under the fences, climb the fences and break them down to get to the mares.

We battled on for a couple of months after the surgery, waiting for the hormones to fall and for him to gain some sense, which he did eventually. Then I was able to appreciate his incredible intelligence and personable character. He needed a lot of mental stimulation or he would come up with all sorts of inappropriate games to play to amuse himself. He would have been an amazing pony to teach tricks to and would have been a fantastic little mascot for the charity, and I did briefly consider keeping him on for that reason. But, my gosh, I did want him off our property, because he just caused havoc all the time.

At one point, my lovely Trav was petrified to leave the yards and go and graze because tiny wee Oscar terrorised him as soon as he stepped into 'his' paddock. Oscar harassed Tansy over the fence and she reared in protest and sliced open her fetlock and the vet had to come to stitch up a vein. One day when we were taking Oscar for a walk through the streets, along with our dogs, he bit one of them on the back. And he also killed one of our chickens that had deigned to walk into his yard.

Needless to say, he was not one of my favourite foster horses, although I was committed to keeping him for as long as it took to find a great home.

Fortunately, the perfect home arrived.

The time had come for me to send my filly, Leila, off for starting under saddle so I booked her in with Ken Faulkner and asked if I could send down Oscar at the same time, for them to do something with him. Oscar was desperate to engage with people and activities and put all that sharp mental aptitude to good use and the trainers down there had a great time with him.

While he was there, he met some devoted natural horsemanship students who were staying for a weekend workshop. They had come from Canada originally and brought their two horses and their dogs with them, which was a pretty good indication of their commitment to a lifelong home for their animals. They fell in love with Oscar and adopted him. And it was Oscar's adopting people who I then approached to ask if they'd like to adopt Bella too.

It was the first time I'd ever tried to handpick a home for a horse, but all the wrong types of people were enquiring about Bella. They wanted her to breed from (and we wouldn't adopt horses into breeding programs) or they wanted her for their child, and she was not a child's pony. That meant there were limited options for her. But I knew Oscar's people would give her a brilliant home for life. And as it turned out, when I emailed them, they'd actually been talking about it anyway. So it was perfect.

By this time I was pregnant, and I didn't want to take on any more foster horses until after I'd had my baby and knew what I could handle. So the only foster horse we had left was Tansy.

A few months after my son was born, I resigned from my position in the charity and Alwyn and I decided we could take just one more horse into our life and that, of course, would be Tansy. The charity officially wound up not long after.

Tansy is still with us. I knew something was wrong when she began rapidly losing weight. She yawned one day while I was standing at her head and I could see straight away that all those top teeth were gone. We'd moved house by this stage and the grass we have now has fewer calories than what we had when we were rescuing horses, which doesn't make it easy to keep weight on a horse like Tansy. The lesser grass quality, combined with her loss of teeth, has meant we now feed Tansy a full Thoroughbred ration each day. (And we feed our two senior citizens, Sparky and Anastasia, nearly as much again.)

Tansy is still young, at thirteen years of age, so she has a long way to go yet. But that's the commitment we made when we took her, and all our animals, so we'll continue to find a way to care for her, just as we will for all the animals in our home and in our hearts.

We do absolutely know now that we've reached the maximum number of horses we're able to support. And maybe it's a good thing our new pastures are of poorer quality, just to prompt us to pull up in our efforts. There are many more horses out there that need help and we will, undoubtedly, rescue more one day, but not until our herd size has naturally decreased and we're practically able to have more again. It's most important to us that we serve along the lines of quality, not quantity. For us, there's no point in rescuing horses if we can't provide them everything they need. At the same time, we know that the animals choose us (just like

Lincoln did), not the other way around; we know there's no need to push.

So, just as Rebel Morrow says, we're not looking.

But, you know, maybe, if the right one comes along (and they always do) . . . then who knows. But we're not looking!

ACKNOWLEDGEMENTS

With heartfelt thanks to every person who is mentioned in these stories, for baring your soul, opening your home, sharing your humour, your sorrow and your immense love for horses, and welcoming me into your paddock and your heart – the honour is truly mine; Penguin for gifting me this great privilege of sharing these stories with the world; Andrea McNamara for inviting me to write the book and for having such faith in my ability to do so; Jo Rosenberg for guiding my words onto the printed page; Louisa Maggio and Grace West for the beautiful design; my agent, Fiona Inglis, for shepherding me through the publishing world; MaryAnne Leighton for making such an important contribution to Nicole and Astro's chapter; Amber Morley and Dianne Smith (both of you sensible and compassionate champions for animals) for reading the first draft and offering valuable feedback; Penguin author Sue Williams for taking time away from her tight deadlines to share some advice; my husband, Alwyn Blayse, who didn't just 'let me' run a charity for three years instead of taking a proper job and making money, but instead strongly advocated for the necessity to do so, for welcoming so many equines into our now very-large family, and for continuing to joyfully spend our vacation money on hay bales and vet bills; the many earth angels who appeared at just the right time to volunteer and work through the charity and help so many horses; and to the many horses I've known and loved, helped, been unable to help, watched get better, watched die, and to whom a piece of my heart is forever attached.

CONTACTS

Alwyn Blayse
Blue Ribbon Physiotherapy
PO Box 155, Kilcoy, QLD, 4515
0410 758 193
blueribbonphysiotherapy@gmail.com

Big Ears Animal Sanctuary (Brett and Jacqui Steele)
PO Box 426, Prospect, TAS, 7250
bj2103@bigpond.com
bigearsanimalsanctuary.com

Elf the Little Grey Pony (Jill Strachan)
Equine Learning for Futures Inc.
info@equinelearningforfutures.com.au
equinelearningforfutures.com.au
Facebook: Elf the Little Grey Pony

Gaye Harvey
Horse Heaven (Croyden Park)
Croyden Park, 144 Bordergate Rd, Cottonvale, QLD, 4375
gaye@horse-heaven.com.au
facebook.com/croydenpark

Horses for Hope Program (Colin Emonson)
PO Box 1697, Shepparton, VIC, 3632
(03) 5831 6157
colin@ucce.org.au
horsesforhope.org.au

Horses Helping Humans (Sue Spence)
horseshelpinghumansaustralia.com

Horse Whispering Youth Program (Sue Spence)
hwyp.com.au

Kelsie Consadine (Soul)
matchplayperformancehorses@gmail.com

MaryAnne Leighton
Author of *Equine Emergency Rescue – a Guide to Large Animal Rescue*
equineER.com

Nicole Graham
Performance Equine Dentistry
PO Box 415, Lara, VIC, 3212
0438 822 704
info@performancedentistry.com.au

Project Hope Horse Welfare Victoria Inc.
GPO Box 1991, Melbourne, VIC, 3001
1300 881 606
phhwv.org.au

Rebel Morrow
rebelmorrow.com
facebook.com/RebelMorrowEventing

RSPCA Tasmania
(03) 6332 8200
rspcatas.org.au

Scilla Sayer
Chiron Horse Programs
Equine-facilitated Therapy, Education and Re-creation
'Wrenshaven', 1491 Huon Road, Leslie Vale, TAS, 7054
scilla.sayer@gmail.com